Sounding the Alarm in the Schoolhouse

Sounding the Alarm in the Schoolhouse

Safety, Security, and Student Well-Being

Nicholas D. Young, Christine N. Michael, and Jennifer A. Smolinski

ROWMAN & LITTLEFIELD
Lanham • Boulder • New York • London

Published by Rowman & Littlefield
An imprint of The Rowman & Littlefield Publishing Group, Inc.
4501 Forbes Boulevard, Suite 200, Lanham, Maryland 20706
www.rowman.com

6 Tinworth Street, London SE11 5AL, United Kingdom

Copyright © 2019 by Nicholas D. Young, Christine N. Michael, and Jennifer A. Smolinski

All rights reserved. No part of this book may be reproduced in any form or by any electronic or mechanical means, including information storage and retrieval systems, without written permission from the publisher, except by a reviewer who may quote passages in a review.

British Library Cataloguing in Publication Information Available

Library of Congress Cataloging-in-Publication Data Is Available

ISBN 978-1-4758-4792-5 (cloth: alk. paper)
ISBN 978-1-4758-4793-2 (pbk: alk. paper)
ISBN 978-1-4758-4794-9 (electronic)

∞™ The paper used in this publication meets the minimum requirements of American National Standard for Information Sciences—Permanence of Paper for Printed Library Materials, ANSI/NISO Z39.48-1992.

Contents

Acknowledgments　vii

Preface　ix

1　The Evolution of School Security: Historical to Contemporary Considerations　1

2　Understanding Variations of Violence: Defining "Safety" in the Schoolhouse　21

3　Crisis in the Classroom: The Mental Health Concerns of Children and Adolescents　41

4　Protocols and Preemptive Preparation: Effective Interventions that Support Students　63

5　Proactive and Protective Programs: Active Engagement to Foster School Safety　77

6　Creating the Peaceable Kingdom: Cultivating Student Well-Being and Connectedness　89

References　119

About the Authors　137

Acknowledgments

We would like to express our gratitude to Sue Clark for her expertise in editing this book. Her dedication, professionalism, and attention to detail made this tome stronger. Her kind demeanor and cheerful disposition also made her a pleasure to work with. She will forever remain a valued friend and colleague.

Preface

Sounding the Alarm in the Schoolhouse: Safety, Security, and Student Well-Being was written as a resource guide for educational and mental health professionals and policymakers, as well as families and communities seeking to develop programming to reduce school violence and promote safe, engaging, and effective schools. This book explores the growing crisis in school safety and security through the lens of the roles that mental health and student and community well-being play in creating environments that are resistant to violent and antisocial behavior. Covering such topics as the burgeoning mental health epidemic among children and teens, family stress and coping, community violence, and the de facto role that schools increasingly play in addressing student health needs, this book presents proactive programming to bolster student health, well-being, and engagement in school activities. It also introduces protocols and preemptive preparation to assist schools in their readiness to intervene in crisis situations.

The book gives practical information and research on school, classroom or community applications, the latest trends and issues in the field, and best practices for promoting student health and well-being. It also covers violence prevention measures and protocols to follow in crisis intervention situations. Issues of culture, gender and society are specifically addressed.

The motivation for writing this book comes from several concerns:

- *Our belief that all students have a right to a safe and secure school environment in which to learn, play, socialize and realize their full potentials;*
- *Our concern about the troubling increases in acts of violence in our schools and on their campuses in recent years;*
- *Our understanding that levels of anxiety, depression, social aggression and other mental health problems are rising in our schools as a result of*

stressors in contemporary life and that if left untreated, these problems may escalate into violent actions;
- *Our recognition that fields such as counseling psychology, developmental psychology, and alternative health and well-being have much to lend to the creation of safe and healthy schools;*
- *Our knowledge that there are proven strategies to bolster students' well-being, self-esteem, sense of connection, self-efficacy, and resiliency in schools and beyond;*
- *Our commitment to viewing schools, families, and community members as an inextricably linked network in supporting school safety and student well-being;*
- *Our awareness that there are alternative forms of student discipline that seem effective in creating equitable systems of justice, teach self-regulation skills, and are transparent and understood by all members of a school's community;*
- *Our belief that all schools must discuss mental health and well-being with students, staff, teachers and families and equip them with the knowledge and skills to promote positive mental health and know how to respond when they have concerns about student health and well-being.*

Unfortunately, there is a long history of school violence in this country that dates to the earliest schools that were established. Violence against both students and teachers has been well-documented in books that chronicle America's educational past. As schools became more diverse and attempted to inculcate citizenry into not only the affluent class, but all children in this country, problems in school safety and student well-being diversified.

This diversity, which has been celebrated as part of America's rich history and current strength, can at times present challenges to our schools. Sadly, too many students from marginalized populations do not find school to be an embracing environment. Acts of violence—large or small, individual or group, face-to-face or cyber, and overt or subtle—can disrupt a productive educational and social environment. Recent national events have forced us to redefine what constitutes "violence" and "safety." The necessity of ensuring emotional, psychological and spiritual safety in school has been joined with concerns over physical safety.

These concerns about the scope of school safety are co-joined with rising concerns over the increase in mental health issues among children and adolescents of school age. It has been estimated by many sources that approximately 20 percent of today's PK-12 students suffer from emotional and psychological stressors and conditions; many more may be undiagnosed, especially in poor and underserved communities (Ngui, Khasakhala, Ndetei, & Roberts, 2010). Mental health problems, emotional instability, family violence, depression, suicidal ideation, and social isolation have been identified in cases of school violence such as attacks and shootings (Paolini, 2015).

Teachers and educational staff are not directly trained to deal with the mental health crisis nor do they have time and skills, given the heavy mandates placed upon contemporary schools, to attend to the many daily observations and check-ins that might alert them to potential crises-in-the-making. Yet, in order to create school communities that have truly safe and nurturing environments, school leaders must begin with the question of how best to promote positive health and well-being in all members of its community.

The safest schools are the ones that understand that policies and protocol regarding school safety must be accompanied by healthy, caring individuals. This applies to both students and educators, as adults in the building set the tone for how students interact with one another, and unhealthy, stressed, or devalued adults often make poor choices in responding to student behavior, model disrespect for others, or do not have the energies to create and sustain meaningful relationships with others.

Beyond creating classrooms that promote genuine relationships, meaningful learning, and collective responsibility for all students' well-being, our schools need to embrace their roles in promoting prosocial behavior, inclusion, and valuing each student so that all are motivated to achieve and feel a connection to their school community. In doing so—in lessening feelings of marginalization, exclusion, victimization or powerlessness—educators and students can help prevent anxiety, depression, disengagement and isolation in the student body. Talking about and directly engaging in school-wide practices that boost wellness and resiliency in and out of the classroom increases the likelihood that a healthy school culture will exist. In the presence of prosocial bonding more students will find their niche and be less likely to need to find antisocial ways of gaining attention.

By reviewing history, research and case studies involving best practice, what can we glean that will help us create safer and more supportive schools? What do fields such as developmental and counseling psychology tell us about how to bolster student well-being and resilience? How do we articulate policies and protocols that ensure cultures of inclusion? How can alternative practices in health, discipline, and classroom management inform our protocols? This book aims to offer some suggestions.

The focal points of the chapters of this book are mentioned previously. We have taken steps to include a balance of research, theory, and well-documented best practice, as we navigate the pressing issues related to developing safe and healthy schools and communities. This book takes a wholistic approach to student security by seeing the connections between and among classroom connections, student engagement, equitable behavioral expectations and disciplinary codes, and school climates that promote prosocial behavior and respect.

Written by experienced PK-12 and higher education professionals, this text attempts to add to the body of literature on how to best approach issues of school safety, from individual, school, and community perspectives. By providing a seminal understanding of some of the current theory and practice behind student mental health, school safety protocols and preparation, supporting school diversity, innovative behavioral interventions, and cross-cultural research on school violence, we hope to empower all of those who are working in PK-12 buildings to create school environments in which students can feel secure, valued, and important to the daily life of the learning community.

Sounding the Alarm in the Schoolhouse: Safety, Security, and Student Well-Being is oriented toward practitioners, providing a truncated review of relevant literature, which is then translated into suggestions to guide practice. We hope that the book serves as a catalyst for exploring student-centered learning and assessment that is founded on solid principles, data, and success stories. With engaged students as the engines of their own learning, schools should see an increase in prosocial behaviors and academic achievement, while diminishing the deleterious effects of disengagement in the schoolhouse.

Chapter 1

The Evolution of School Security
Historical to Contemporary Considerations

School violence is by no means a new phenomenon. There are recorded accounts of violent activities in American schools that date back as far as the first schools themselves. Newman (1980, as cited in Smith, Morita, Junger-Tas, Catalano, Olweus, & Slee, 1999) provides one of the most comprehensive overviews of school disturbance in America that illustrates how old a concept this is

> as late as the seventeenth century, children participated in acts that, if committed in modern times, would result in not only their being defined as delinquent but also in requiring their parents and other adults to be charged with contributing to their delinquency. As soon as they could talk, most children learned and used obscene language and gestures; many engaged in sexual activity at an early age, willingly or otherwise; they drank freely in taverns, if not at home; few of them ever went to school, and when they did, they wore sidearms, participated in brawls, and fought duels. (p. 7)

It was not until the notion of childhood as a distinct developmental phase in the life cycle evolved and was recognized, with new norms and expectations, that behaviors that seemed perfectly acceptable at home, in school, and in the larger society began to be viewed as somewhat deviant or abnormal (Crews & Counts, 1997). Certainly, one major role of early schools was to inculcate a more socially acceptable code of conduct; yet, disturbance in schools in the United States colors the history of American education in every decade of our country's existence.

Interestingly, as Crews & Counts (1997) note, the earliest recordings of school violence focus on corporal punishment by teachers against their students. It was perfectly common in Jesuit schools in the 1600s to expect physical disciplining of students. Serious offenses were met with students being stripped in front of the entire school community and whipped until they bled. Beatings and whippings were standard teaching tools (Crews & Counts, 1997).

A BRIEF HISTORY OF VIOLENCE IN AMERICAN SCHOOLS

As early as April 30, 1866, an editorial in the *New York Times* wrote in protest of students carrying pistols to school, expressing concern about possible accidental or intentional school shootings (K12 Academics, 2018). The first documented mass shooting involving American students took place in 1891, when a seventy-year-old discharged his gun into a group of students on the playground of St. Mary's Parochial School in Newburgh, New York (Del Giudice, 2018). There were only minor injuries to several of the students, yet this occurrence was rare, given that most school disturbances during this period involved student-on-student violence or violence against teachers and stones and knives were the weapons of choice (K12 Academics, 2018).

According to the K12 Academics (2018), on March 6, 1884, in Boston, Massachusetts, the first "copycat" violence was seen, as news of Jesse James reached the East Coast and students held fort in the Concord-street schoolhouse, fashioning themselves as another Jesse James Gang. A group of officers investigated, and in their attempt to escape, one member of the "gang" accidently fired at an officer. Several boys were captured; however, the shooter and several others got away (Del Giudice, 2018).

17th and 18th Century School Disturbance

Religion was the primary influence on education in 17th- and 18th-century America. Schools were the major vehicle for religious recruitment and their mission was to instill morals and values in students (Midlarsky & Klain, 2005). Parents receiving educational materials were told to discipline their children, to avoid pampering them, train them for hard work and teach them to be respectful of and obedient to all forms of authority (Midlarsky & Klain, 2005). Despite the heavy religious impress, school violence still occurred during the Colonial times.

According to Crews & Counts (1997) Colonial education was essentially a disorganized affair that had few regulations and was not carried out continuously. This was due to the fact that the states owned public schools and regulated them, relying completely on community taxes in order to run them. Each community organized its own school, which was compulsory only for children of certain ages. Much greater attention was paid to educating boys—a fact that the authors see as rather remarkable as education was not seen as requisite for career advancement and training, other than for the ministry (Midlarsky & Klain, 2005).

Midlarsky & Klain (2005) view the rampant violence in Colonial schools as mirroring the social and political turbulence of the time. Violence was directed mostly against school masters, who were required to be of physical size and stature to combat the protests and aggressive actions of the older male students (Midlarsky & Klain, 2005). The authors note that there were over 300 reported student mutinies that occurred annually, with the direct result being headmasters driven out of their schoolhouses by their students.

There was a four-pronged approach to Colonial education that included family members, the church, schools, and the press as surrogate school masters. In 1842, the Compulsory Education Act required that parents become legally responsible for their children's education; that education was to consist of capital laws, reading, and religion (Crews & Counts, 1997). If a community was larger in number than 50, it must also offer reading and writing instruction; grammar schools were mandated in communities with a population of 100 or more (Crews & Counts, 1970).

Colonial children were instructed in religion at home and were involved in apprenticeships that paved the way to their eventual careers. Children most commonly apprenticed with a master for a period of seven years, during which they learned not only a vocational skill, but rudimentary math, reading, and writing; however, in the many occurrences of labor shortages during this time period, their educations were often interrupted or cut short (Crews & Counts, 1997).

Colonial education was shaped by the Church and the invention of the printing press. The fundamental purpose of reading and writing instruction was to prepare people to read the Bible and other religious tracts. The printing press leveled the educational playing field because with its inception, all classes of individuals, even children, could have access to materials once reserved only for the elite (Crews & Counts, 1997). With this newfound access to learning materials, Colonists now shifted to the belief that more than those destined for the clergy needed a formal liberal arts education (Crews & Counts, 1997).

Those who were fortunate enough to attend a grammar school learned Latin grammar, conversation and composition, Greek and Hebrew grammar, and were exposed to Greek and Latin literature (Crews & Counts, 1997). There was a distinct separation between the types of schooling that children could access based upon their socioeconomic class. The children of the elite could attend the private dame schools while children of the lower classes went to the town schools or worked as apprentices (Crews & Counts, 1997).

The middle colonies, according to Crews & Counts (1997), developed models of school that were different from the aforementioned grammar schools of New England. Students could attend one of three models to include church, entrepreneurial, or charity (Crews & Counts, 1997). Church schools stood by denomination but many allowed children from other religious groups to attend if they lived in close geographical proximity. Urban areas were more populated by the entrepreneurial schools, which were modeled on businesses and advertised and sold their wares. These schools prepared students for valuable careers such as engineering, navigation, and surveying. Charity schools were instituted as free schools that served poor children and orphans.

Immigration patterns, high mortality rates, and instability among family patterns caused the South to be far behind other parts of the country in its schooling (Crews & Counts, 1997). Southern schools saw their primary mission as spreading the Gospel, teaching children math and writing to the degree that they could find employment, and bolstering reading ability in order to comprehend the Scriptures (Crews & Counts, 1997). The South also had distinct "old field schools"; the schools were literally placed in dormant fields and run by teachers who often were completely unfit and uneducated. Cubberly (1962) remarked that many were drunks or physically abused their pupils.

The National Period

The National Period (1780–1860) saw schools become agents of republicanism, transmitting such virtues as discipline, sacrifice, living a life of simplicity, and intelligence (Midlarsky & Klain, 2005). Despite the inculcation of such values, students in schools continued to be disciplinary problems and over 400 schools were ruined by violent student behavior (Horace Mann, 1934 as cited by Midlarsky & Klain, 2005). Colleges were equally chaotic, with fights, fires, and protests.

There were differing opinions during the National Period as to what the true purpose of the nation's schools should be; for example, some individuals felt that schools should not be in the business of promoting specific moral or political views; rather, that education should prepare individuals to make independent decisions and was to prepare the next generation of leaders (Crews & Counts, 2005).

To this end, young men suited to leadership were to be identified early in life and educated through their college years; however, individuals such as Noah Webster saw schools in the more traditional role of inculcating patriotism and moral values; thus, he was instrumental in developing the American Bible, dictionaries, and standard spelling books (Crews & Counts, 1997).

By 1830, Joseph Lancaster had put in place systems to school the huge numbers of America's urban poor. This system, known as monitorial, jammed upward of several hundred to a thousand students into a single classroom (Crews & Counts, 1997). The monitors cruised the rows of students, who were separated by their academic ability levels. This system had the benefit of being efficient and cheap, but it was nowhere near an ideal model to develop critical thinkers, problem solvers, or creative individuals (Crews & Counts, 1997).

It was during the Industrial Revolution that school became a regular and important part of the daily life of American children. Schools, it was felt, were the tools to socialize unruly children into productive citizenry; however, school violence threatened to interfere with this mission; the lack of knowledge about effective and engaging teaching, antisocial student behaviors, and poor classroom management techniques produced chaos in the classroom (Crews & Counts, 1997).

One of the earliest school shooters, Matthew Ward of Louisville, Kentucky, killed his schoolmaster because he perceived that the punishment meted out against his brother was too harsh. Even though the murder was committed in full view of others, he was eventually acquitted (K12 Academics, 2018).

The 20th Century

At the turn of the century, waves of immigrants came to America and each one influenced education in the schoolhouse. The "Gary Plan" was instituted to address this trend; similar to Dewian beliefs, students engaged in a three-pronged educational approach that included work, study, and play (Cohn & Mohl, 1979). There was intense student backlash, however, especially among the immigrant population, against the changes that so many felt would impede their ability to learn and assimilate into American culture (Crews & Counts, 1997). There were strikes, political protests and other acts of violence perpetrated by students. Those students who did not become engaged in the movement frequently were targeted and beaten (Cohn & Mohl, 1979).

The 1930s saw a new innovation—that of the disciplinary classroom where, in the face of infractions, students were placed as punishment (Crews & Counts, 1997). At this point in educational history, teachers did not spend much time or effort in individualizing academic work or crafting behavioral plans for individual students. Students were expected to behave, and if the disciplinary classrooms did not produce behavioral improvement, students were sent to "parental schools" (Crews & Counts, 1997). These were schools of last resort, and if offenders did not mend their ways, they were forced out of the public school system and sent instead to state industrial schools (Crews & Counts, 1997).

Such industrial schools became the method of choice for combating student behavioral problems; in the early 1930s, one out of every 350 students had been sent to an industrial school where they were separated by gender, and in the South, there was also racial segregation (Cubberly, 1934). If one were not trained to prosocial behavior, his or her last stop was the penitentiary for youthful offenders, and according to Cubberly (1934), so many students were sent there that the penitentiaries became a de facto wing of the public education system.

The biggest issues in school disturbance during the 1930s and 1940s were truancy and vagrancy, with teachers also voicing frustration with students not respecting authority, acting in immoral or dishonest ways, failing to take their studies seriously, and displaying disorderly conduct (Cubberly, 1934). As might be expected, they cited boys as having far more behavioral issues than girls.

Boys, it was believed, were predisposed to bond with other boys; while friendship and adventure were the primary goals of these friendships, there were concerns that, given the nature of masculinity, these bands of boys would compete against each other, trying to top each other's behaviors (Douglass, 1940). The concept of a "gang" mentality, leading to possible risky behavior, arose for the first time in educational conversations (Douglass, 1940).

A more sociological approach to student behavior took hold, with students given batteries of tests, as well as physical exams and reviews of home life factors (Douglass, 1940). Educators now considered the influence of adverse childhood events such as unexpected loss, divorce or separation as possibly contributing to violent behavior (Douglass, 1940).

The 1940s saw a rash of international conflicts, the Great Depression and world war. In the face of these troubles, student disruption diminished. Behavioral issues tended to be very minor, such as chewing gum, littering, running in the hallways and being too noisy (Crews & Counts, 1997). The classroom teaching methodologies became heavily influenced by the military, and a large number of teachers left for military service of one kind or another.

Briefly, following the war, teachers saw their status become elevated in society as the United States attempted to make speedy advances in their science and technology abilities (Crews & Counts, 1997). Schools were able to recruit more educated personnel, pay improved, and better teaching methods and materials meant that students' classrooms became more engaging.

The 1950s saw a rise in the occurrences of student violence, amid a period during which there was emphasis on positive citizenship and maintaining "The American Way." This hinted at things to come in the next decade, when there were explosions of student protests and violence (Crews & Counts, 1997). Generally, the most common reports of school disturbance were for lack of responsibility, stealing, lack of respect for authority and other such misbehaviors (Crews & Counts, 1997). Brewing below the surface, however, were the movements that would shape and define the 1960s and 1970s; social movements such as civil rights and the anti-war movements.

During 1960s the term "school violence" was invented, amid a period that saw increases in assaults on teachers and weapons offenses and 200 deaths were classified in a school year (Midlarsky & Klain, 2005). The 1960s and 1970s brought much turmoil to American schools; schools reflected the racial and civil rights battles seen in the larger society. For students of color and their families, American schools were seen as places that did not reflect their contributions to history nor celebrate their unique place in America's landscape (Midlarsky & Klain, 2005). Their frustrations spilled over into actions that frequently became violent. Court-ordered desegregation, in which students were bused outside of their communities to achieve racial balance in school systems, also contributed to these turbulent times (Midlarsky & Klain, 2005).

Other communities, such as "Southie" in Boston, fought back, with whites demonstrating violently against students of color who were forced into integrating what traditionally had been white, Italian, and Irish neighborhoods. Buses were stoned, students were spat upon, and ugly racial slurs were hurled as these changes took place (Gellerman, 2014). Many students of color feared for their lives on a daily basis. This prompted many to arm themselves in an attempt to be safe at schools and when traveling to and from these unfamiliar communities (Gellerman, 2014).

Crews & Counts (1997) gave the 1960s the moniker of "the kaleidoscopic era" due to the rapid shifts in social and educational policy. Student disruptions now moved into much more deadly territory with murder, robbery, and other forms of violence taking place during protests (Crews & Counts, 1997). Television amplified our ability to see firsthand the inequalities, inequities, and injustices that existed in society, galvanizing students to protest to address their own or others' needs (Crews & Counts, 1997).

During the 1970s, the annual Gallup Poll reflected that school violence was among the top ten national concerns (Midlarsky & Klain, 2005). Between the years of 1970 and 1973, there were documented increases in all categories of school violence, including homicides, rapes, assaults on teachers, possession of weapons on school grounds, and targeted bullying (Crews & Counts, 1997). It was the first time in our country's history that students were at greater risk of encountering violence in their schools than in any other location (Midlarsky & Klain, 2005).

During the 1980s, four different national reports lambasted the state of American education; the first was the landmark *A Nation at Risk* (Kamenetz, 2018). While the reports focused on the poor quality of teaching, leadership, low standards, and dismal student performance, the country was undergoing massive cuts to social service and education programs at a time when rates of child abuse and neglect and delinquent behavior were on the uptick (Kamenetz, 2018). The behavior of K-12 students led 33 percent of this nation's teachers to report that they were seriously considering exiting the teaching profession. Street and school crime increased, with the same numbers of attacks on adolescents happening in both locales (Crews & Counts, 1997).

Educators linked the increase in school violence to a number of school-related and nonschool variables, including increasing school and class sizes, tension between schools and parents, crumbling and aged school environments, and an unwillingness to report or follow due process when crimes took place (Crews & Counts, 1997).

Sociological and economic factors were blamed for the increase in school violence. Violence was the result of the growing number of single-parent households, an ineffective juvenile justice system, bad student morale, social media, decreased parental involvement in schools, and police mishandling of students. With the erosion of home, community, and societal supports, many schools reinvented themselves into "full service" schools, providing such services as medical care, nutrition, dental care, social services, counseling, and parent education in the same complex or building as the actual school (Crews & Counts, 1997).

Gang violence spilled over from the streets to the school grounds. The rise of drugs, particularly crack cocaine, is blamed for most of the turf wars, as gangs fought to control their territories and business interests. Gangs had found their way into 50 percent of the largest urban schools; Miller (1975) reported in one of the earliest studies that there were at least 2,300 different gangs active in the United States. Eventually, these gangs migrated from urban areas into suburban and rural school districts too (Miller, 1975).

The increase in gang activity and other expressions of violence resulted in some 20 percent of students carrying a weapon to school in the 1990s, according to Crews & Counts (1997). Between 1997 and 1998, there were sixty school-related deaths (forty-eight homicides and twelve suicides) and eighty-three out of every thousand American teachers was a victim of a crime (Crews & Counts, 1997). In 1997, Michael Carneal shot and killed three students while wounding others; this West Paducah, Kentucky attack engendered one of the earliest debates over a possible connection between certain mental health diagnoses and school violence (Langman, 2015). Carneal, who pleaded guilty to mental illness rather than to murder, was imprisoned for life (Langman, 2015).

The Event that was Columbine

On April 20, 1999, students Eric Harris, 18, and Dylan Klebold, 17, shot students and teachers at Columbine High School in Littleton, Colorado, killing twelve classmates and a teacher and wounding twenty-six others, taking their own lives in the school's library (Langman, 2015). For many in this country, televised images from that massacre are the first vivid memories of school violence and they launched a national crusade to better protect students in our schools. Frighteningly, subsequent shooters often have cited Harris and Klebold as their role models and were very familiar with their writings and plans (Pfeifer & Gansevoort, 2014).

The Columbine shootings became etched in memory because, for the first time, there were so many artifacts left behind by the killers; there were writings done as school assignments, journals, and the infamous Basement Tapes (Langman, 2015). Books were written by survivors, parents, and researchers, most notably the 400-plus-page tome by Dave Cullen, simply entitled *Columbine*. Numerous reports and official documents eventually were released, but there still continues to be debate about the motives and the psychology behind the killings (Langman, 2015).

21st-Century Violence

The 21st century feels, at times, as though it has been dominated by school shootings. Ahmed & Walker (2018) note school shootings that took place in the first twenty-one weeks of 2018, including those in Noblesville, Indiana; Santa Fe, Texas (10 fatalities); Palmdale, California; Ocala, Florida; Lexington Park, Maryland; and Birmingham, Alabama. Their statistics show that attacks occurred in every geography and at all school levels. The authors estimate approximately one shooting a week on average during 2018.

Del Giudice (2018) chronicled some of the more prominent acts of school violence that have taken place in recent years.

- On Valentine's Day of 2018, a former student shot and killed seventeen people at Marjory Stoneman Douglas High School in Parkland, Florida. This act ignited student protests in favor of gun control around the country.
- Preceding this act in 2018, two students were killed and fourteen wounded by gunfire when a student opened fire prior to the beginning of classes at Marshall County High School in west Kentucky.
- On September 13, 2017, a fifteen-year-old boy was killed at Freeman High School in Rockford, Washington, and three female students were wounded when another fifteen-year-old boy opened fire with a handgun.
- Perhaps the most wrenching of school shootings took place on December 14, 2012, when a twenty-year-old gunman killed twenty first-grade children and six educators inside Sandy Hook Elementary School in Newtown, Connecticut. The shooter then took his own life. After the incident, it was discovered that he also had fatally shot his mother before entering the school.

- The Sandy Hook incident galvanized public outcry about the ease of obtaining weapons and of entering our nation's schools, prompting some to begin the discussion about arming teachers and other school personnel.

These incidents have heightened both awareness of the need for new approaches to school security and the fear that schools are no longer the safe havens they were created to be. While there may be many different explanations for the rise in school violence; several are considered here.

THE RISE OF MENTAL HEALTH ISSUES AMONG SCHOOL-AGE CHILDREN

It is estimated by several credible sources that at least 20 percent of school-aged children in this country have mental health issues (Anderson, 2016; Mahnken, 2017). Between the years of 2010 and 2015 there was a 50 percent increase in the number of children hospitalized for self-injuring and hospitalizations for mood disorders among children and teens rose dramatically, as have calls to suicide hotlines (Page, 2017). Research indicates both that children's mental health issues are growing and that the numbers who need help and are not receiving it are expanding (Friedrich, Mendez, & Mihalas, 2010).

The estimated number of children under the age of eighteen with mental, behavioral or emotional disorders is approximately 15 million in the United States alone; tragically, only about 50 percent are afforded either medication or psychological services and fewer than 10 percent of adolescents say that they have been served by a mental health professional in the past year (Mahnken, 2017). Hoagwood, Burns, Kiser, Ringeisen, and Schoenwalkd (2001) have put the figure as high as 70–80 percent when they write of the numbers of students receiving mental health services from schools only.

The documented number of students diagnosed with ADHD, conduct disorders, depression, autism, and substance abuse continues to escalate, yet fewer families have the means to cover their children's treatment; thus, school systems are left to serve as de facto mental health providers (Mahnken, 2017). Children who suffer mental health problems without treatment are at much greater risk to develop future problems such as criminal activity, substance abuse, and dropping out of school.

Schools alone cannot combat this trend. While the National Association of School Psychologists (NASP) (2015) promotes a ratio of one psychologist for every 700 students, the actual ratio is double that figure. As school mandates and other initiatives skyrocket, it is impossible for school personnel also to fill the role of counselor effectively. With the dearth of personnel equipped to act in the roles of mental health counselors, it is increasingly likely that mental health and emotional issues will continue to play out in incidents of school disruption. The topic of student mental health and its relation to school safety and security is discussed in greater detail in upcoming chapters.

Mental Health and School Violence

Konnikova (2014), writing in *The New Yorker*, uses the case of Marysville, Washington shooter Jaylen Fryberg to illustrate the debate that arises with each incidence of school violence in our country, which is, are gun violence (and other violent actions) and mental health related? And are there warning signs in these cases that could have prevented tragedy? Ostensibly, Fryberg was a "good kid": popular, involved in athletics, volunteering in his community. The week before he went on a shooting rampage, he was chosen prince of the school's homecoming court (Konnikova, 2014).

Yet, as Konnikova (2014) reports, as so often is the case in recent incidents, tweets, texts, Instagram and Facebook messages and posts show a very different portrait—one of an anguished individual whose mental health was suffering. Public perception reveals that the majority of people in recent years believe that mass shootings are the result of a failed mental health system (Konnikova, 2014).

The most current research discovered that the association between severe forms of mental illness (psychosis or a major mood disorder) and violent actions were low (13 percent); however, the likelihood of acting violently depended greatly on whether other factors such as unemployment, living in poverty, abusing substances or living in disadvantaged communities were present (Swanson et al., 2016). Adding two of these factors doubled the risk and adding three raised the risk of violence to 30 percent (Swanson et al., 2016). Swanson and his team (2016) found that the occurrence of violence was more closely related to being male, poor, and abusing drugs or alcohol; these three factors alone predicted violent behavior with or without any mental illness.

Other studies, both nationally and internationally, also found a steady but low risk of violence among the mentally ill; however, the addition of other factors, mentioned previously, does increase the risk (Konnikova, 2014). Adolescent males who were substance abusers and loners had the most predictive factors for acting violently, while the mere presence of a diagnosis of a mental illness had little predictive value (Konnikova, 2014). The one important exception that runs through all of the data—violence against oneself (Konnikova, 2014).

It is estimated that between 21 and 44 percent of those who take their own lives had exhibited mental health issues in the past (Swanson et al., 2015). There is a higher risk for suicide among the mentally ill with up to ten to twenty times higher than the general population if an individual suffers from bipolar disorder or depression and thirteen times higher for those with schizophrenia (Swanson et al., 2015). While the large majority of people diagnosed with a mental illness will never act violently, mental illness is strongly connected to an increased risk of suicide, and suicide accounts for over half of the firearms-related fatalities in this country (Swanson et al., 2015). Suicide as a resolution of depression, as in the case of Dylan Klebold at Columbine High School, can be nested inside larger acts of violence against others; however, identifying all cases of depression and other disorders and then predicting who may act out violently against others in the future, remains far from a science (Swanson et al., 2015).

Riggio (2018) sees that mental illness has been the go-to initial explanation for school shootings, citing the earliest descriptions of Santa Fe, Texas shooter Dimitrios Pagourtzis as a psychopath because he kept to himself. One student mentioned, as an example, that Dimitrios was always wearing weird trench coats and looked odd (Riggio, 2018). The danger in such growing stereotyping is that it is not only inaccurate but leads to further isolation of individuals who may need help or connection based solely on observable differences from the perceived school and societal norm.

Swanson (2011) discovered that the greatest predictive factor in future violence was the presence of past violence; and not necessarily major in effect. Minor disputes, what Swanson (2011) called "trait anger," animal cruelty, and other indicators such as multiple DUI's or minor brushes with authority (inside and outside of school) are better predictors of future problems than mental health diagnoses (Swanson, 2011).

There is little question that exposure to violence at school presents a mental health problem for contemporary students. Flannery, Wester, and Singer (2004) studied the relationship between exposure to violence at school and children's reports of symptoms of psychological trauma and violent behavior such as witnessing beatings, students being punched or slapped, and other physical attacks. After the authors had accounted for demographic effects, they found that children and adolescents who were exposed to high levels of violence at school (either witnessing or being victimized themselves) were significantly more likely to experience clinical levels of trauma than those who were exposed to little to no violence (Flannery et al., 2004).

Exposure to violence in general puts students at higher risk for perpetrating aggressive behaviors themselves (Flannery et al., 2004). This is true of any setting in which the violence is experienced—school, home, or community; there are serious and consequential mental health outcomes for those exposed to such violence. The earlier a child is exposed to such violence, the greater the chance of long-term, negative outcomes in mental health and behavior (Flannery et al., 2004). Exposure to high levels of violence and bullying at school corresponded positively to increased depression, anxiety, anger and dissociation, while feelings of powerlessness to help victims result, and students may become hypervigilant, worried that they will become the next victim (Flannery et al., 2004).

The authors suggest that in order to increase mental health and well-being in our schools, school personnel and counselors need to recognize the effects of witnessing school violence as well as to develop and integrate programming that directly addresses the needs of both victims and perpetrators. Whole school wellness can come only if we are cognizant of the long-term effects of exposure to school violence, especially if the exposure is frequent and persists over time.

Possible Causes of School Violence

There are a number of theories as to the possible causes of school violence, especially in considering the cases of school shooters. One theory, that has not received clear cut validation, is that excessive time playing violent video games can lead to such violence (Ferguson, 2008; Sicart, 2009). It is impossible to truly arrive at a conclusion as ethics prevent researchers from testing the link between excessive violent gaming and real-world acts of violence, yet arguments often center on the numbing effect of the such gaming; but again, there is no clear-cut evidence to support them (Sicart, 2009; Twenge, 2012). A meta-analysis conducted by Ferguson (2008) found no evidence that these games, even played excessively, lead to violence, aggressive behavior or school shootings.

Social isolation or outright rejection is another common cause cited in school shooting cases; there is more evidence to support this claim (Leary, Kowalski, Smith, & Phillips, 2003). In the study of fifteen such cases, rejection or victimization were characteristics; however, this is not always as simple as it appears (Leary et al., 2003). Many attributed the Columbine attack on victimization and bullying of the perpetrators, yet this theory is turned on its head by perhaps the most thorough and scholarly study of the case (Cullen, 2009). It is also possible that victimization or rejection is perceived, rather than actual, in the instance of those who commit the acts (Cullen, 2009).

One consistent theme plays a role in the analyses of school shooters- they are deficient in conflict resolution skills, lack empathy for their victims, and wrestle with managing their anger and antisocial emotions (Palumbo, 2016). Once aggrieved, they appear to spiral into a state marked by several repetitive stages: perceived victimization; anger; depression; and then relegation to a permanent state of anger (Palumbo, 2016).

School climate is also blamed for violent actions. In schools in which there is a concerted effort to build community, inclusion, and valuing of all members, there is less likely to be aggression in any form (Benbenishty, Astor, Roziner, & Wrabel, 2016). The larger the school, the harder it is to build that sense of true community unless large institutions are broken down into smaller units or "houses" that foster connection (Benbenishty et al., 2016).

Leary et al. (2003) found a cluster of factors that escalated the risk of violent behavior in students to include acute or chronic rejection, expressed through ostracism, bullying, and/or romantic rejection of the shooters. The shooters were characterized by one or more of three other risk factors such as an interest in firearms or bombs, a fascination with death or Satanism, or psychological problems involving depression, impulse control, or sadistic tendencies (Leary et al., 2003).

Profiles of School Shooters

Intrigued by the fact that the majority of school shootings in this country have taken place more frequently in communities with strong religious populations, they examined the shooters' expressions on existential topics—death, isolation, meaning, personal freedom, and identity (Pfeifer & Ganzevoort, 2014). Using Bailey's (1999) definition of "implicit religion" (religiosity in general) as opposed to explicit, specific types of religion, it is noted that these can differ tremendously and that those who adhere to either assume that their thoughts and beliefs related to each are inherently true.

Pfeifer & Ganzevoort (2014) present an interesting review of the existential concerns of school shooters prior to committing their crimes. Examining their writings, posts, video clips, suicide letters and diary entries, the authors conducted a narrative analysis in order to shed more light on their motives and found that a concern with death, suicide, and murder were frequently discussed (Pfeifer & Ganzevoort, 2014). Isolation is mentioned often, and the shooters discuss feeling lonely, rejected, and treated like they are social outcasts (Pfeifer & Ganzevoort, 2014). Identity is clearly a struggle, with most of the shooters feeling as though they are superior beings whose superiority is not recognized by larger society (Pfeifer & Ganzevoort, 2014).

According to the authors, school shooters appear to believe that they have the right to eliminate those they deem inferior; "natural selection" is a term used by more than one, and they often reference their God-like status and cite this as motivation—a kind of Divine Retribution (Pfeifer & Ganzevoort, 2014). Revenge is also discussed as their motivation for violent actions, and the notion of killing others appears linked to feelings of power (Pfeifer & Ganzevoort, 2014).

Pfeifer & Ganzevoort (2014) write that the feelings of isolation from others around them gives both a rationale for seeking their deaths and a cover for their actions, since as they withdraw from those in their school and family, their actions are less scrutable; however, personal laments about being lonely and rejected do not always match up with external facts. Dylan Harris, for example, wrote about having no money, happiness or friends; yet research showed that he came from a comfortable and caring family background, held a job, and had friends at school (Cullen, 2009).

Another existential concern is that the shooters feel they do not have freedom in their personal lives; rather, they are controlled by social forces, teachers, their parents, and the law (Pfeifer & Ganzevoort, 2014). Equating freedom with absolute control over all aspects of their lives, they abdicate responsibility to others. Ultimately, the greatest freedom is deciding who lives and who dies. Weapons make them feel more confident and in control of their fate, including the decision to take their own lives (Pfeifer & Ganzevoort, 2014).

Pfeifer & Ganzevoort's (2014) analysis echoes many of the same findings of noted scholar Langman (2009), who has written extensively on school shootings for more than a decade and sought to discover if there were mental health indicators that gave clues to their actions. Langman (2009) writes of typologies of school shooters, which are different but may co-exist. The categories include psychopaths, schizophrenics, traumatized shooters, and individuals with schizotypal personality disorders, with clear commonalities among them to include suffering from depression and suicidal thoughts (Langman, 2009). As with the other research, Langman (2009) did not find the shooters to be loners.

Beyond the typologies, the shooters held some characteristics in common; the failure of empathy, noting "to kill innocent people at close range—including classmates and acquaintances—requires a profound lack of feeling for fellow human beings" (Langman, 2009, p. 139). The most common cause of the failure of empathy was the presence of anger that allowed those who acted violently to feel justified in their actions (Langman, 2009).

The shooters' lack of empathy emanated a feeling of "us versus them" or "us against the world" view. Those whom the shooters saw as different were described in their writings and other artifacts as "others," "zombies," or "aliens" (Langman, 2009). The "others" were less than human, while the shooters viewed themselves as a superior human race and all expressed intense anger and experienced existential rage, but their rage differed in origin (Langman, 2009). These different origins might include being compared unfavorably to others, loathing that others "controlled them," having to submit to authority figures, feeling like outcasts, or being tired of being perceived as being victimized (Langman, 2009).

Langman (2009) found that their existential angst often resulted in suicidal thoughts and ideation. Some of the shooters had suffered these feelings for years and had expressed suicidal plans in their artifacts; they documented their feelings of hopelessness and believed that suicide was the only way out (Langman, 2009). Whatever the plan, all the shooters intended to take others with them before ending their own lives.

Langman (2009) also discovered that they were extremely reactive in nature, experiencing murderous rage when they believed that they were being teased, rejected, or slighted socially. While other students their age could slough these insults off, or respond, giving "tit for tat," the shooters quickly escalated emotionally to a point from which they could not dampen down their over-reactions (Langman, 2015).

With their identities so fragile, their reactions to slights—real or imagined—were completely out of proportion to the incidents. The result of these escalated emotions, which developed over a number of years, was a form of self-loathing that further exacerbated their vulnerabilities (Langman, 2015). Since almost all school shooters are males, Langman (2015) notes the connection between rage, depression, and a sense of failed manhood.

Expanding the Notion of Safety, Security, and Violence

Once synonymous with physical well-being, notions of students' safety in school have grown to include socio-emotional and psychological domains, as well, with this expanded definition encompassing the spiritual life of students, their sense of connection to school and the surrounding community, and their feelings of being valued as contributing members of the learning community.

In a small, but fascinating mixed methods study of students' perceptions of safety, Pipe (2014) explored children's mental health and sense of safety in schools. Students were interviewed to see where they felt safe and unsafe, and a total of seven themes were reported (Pipe, 2014). A frequent description of a safe setting was where students had placed themselves in a physical location near trusted friends; thus, connection and proximity to those they considered trustworthy was a key factor in perceived safety (Pipe, 2014). This theme was expanded to include trusted teachers and other school personnel with whom the children had positive connections (Pipe, 2014).

Students, who were given the opportunity to photograph places that they considered safe, also took photos of the front of the school and places within the school, such as the principal's office ("he's a very nice principal"), where they felt they would not experience harm (Pipe, 2014). One student explained a photo of the front of the school by saying "um, the front of the school. Safe. Because I grew up at the school pretty much," (Pipe, p. 27). Clearly, school environment, positive leadership, and a familiarity with the welcoming culture of the school bolstered students' sense of well-being.

On the other hand, unsafe environments included places where there could be physical harm (electrical room, janitor's office), but most often, the places in which bullying or other physical or psychological assaults might occur (Pipe, 2014). One, the students labeled "the bloody corner"; it was the far end of the school yard, and students were aware that assaults and drug use occurred there (Pipe, 2014). Students also mentioned any place where there was an absence of teacher supervision such as at the edges of the school yard, where messages and threats were spray painted in graffiti, warning students of hostility against them (Pipe, 2014).

In short, students relied upon feelings of connection, adult protection, and welcoming environment to provide a base of safety from which they could learn and development (Pipe, 2014). Conversely, when they experienced or feared physical aggression, intimidation and threats, or unacceptable social behavior (such as drug use), they were less secure (Pipe, 2014). Witnessing acts of violence, and even hearing second-hand about such acts, also increased their sense of being unsafe. Students mentioned feeling anxious, sad or stressed daily or weekly if they felt that they had been victimized or might experience victimization (Pipe, 2014).

Pipe's (2014) work demonstrates that schools must take a wholistic view of what makes up a secure environment. When students are bereft of strong connections with friends, teachers, and other school members, their sense of safety and security at school suffers—in some cases, to the point where concerns about personal security override any abilities to learn and interact. This study and others (Duckett, Kagan, & Sixsmith, 2010; Matthews, Demsey, & Overstreet, 2009) suggest the need for developing school security plans in overarching ways that far outstrip the installation of metal detectors, hiring of security guards, or searching student backpacks.

Attention must also be given to creating safety through community and neighborhood partnerships.

CONSIDERING STUDENTS' SOCIO-EMOTIONAL WELL-BEING AS A COMPONENT OF SCHOOL SECURITY

The issue of student well-being as a protective factor for the school community is important enough that the World Health Organization, or WHO, (2003) authored a substantial document that begins by defining a health psycho-social environment as one that takes pride in learning, is friendly and warm; values cooperation over competition; has open, supportive communication; values creativity; eschews physical punishment and prevents harassment, bullying, and violence through nonviolent interactions and protocols;

promotes equal rights among students; and works to promote prosocial environments through education of students and their families.

The 2003 WHO report concludes that a positive social environment at school is integrally related to student behavior. Indicators of alienation and disengagement from school are linked to health compromising behaviors such as substance abuse, smoking and acting antisocially. School connectedness decreased risky behaviors. That feeling of belonging, good communications with school personnel, and the belief that adults in the building care about them improve students' mental, physical, and emotional well-being and can decrease general and school anxiety and emotional and psychosomatic imbalance (WHO, 2003).

A supportive school environment not only makes academic achievement more likely but increases the chance that students will use the school's resources to their advantage. One document provides a Psycho-Social Environment (PSE) profile for schools to use in gauging the positive, supportive factors in a school's environment, as well as areas for improvement (WHO, 2003). The intended outcomes result in school environments that promote health and well-being and drastically reduce the incidents of risky, antisocial, or violent behaviors, both in school and in the surrounding community. The list includes

- to grow toward a whole-school culture that has a healthy, supportive climate;
- uses cooperative learning and problem solving;
- links school and home resources; engages parents;
- forbids any use of physical punishment and violence, as well as verbal equivalents;
- has a zero tolerance policy against all forms of bullying, harassment, and discrimination;
- values and rewards creative activities; and
- gives students emotional and social support so that they develop the confidence to speak freely about their lives in school and actively participate in change initiatives. (WHO, 2003)

Wilke and Fraser (2009) translated many of these concepts into strategies to reduce school violence. Like others, they believe that school attachment and connection to other members of the school community is paramount; thus, schools need to consider a variety of activities—school day and extracurricular—that foster a sense of self-worth and belonging (Wilke & Fraser, 2009). Intentional programs to prevent bullying and increase social skills are also necessary, as are venues for students to voice their concerns and share problems they are having in an anonymous way (Wilke & Fraser, 2009).

Resources for alienated or rejected students, or those who are in marginalized and target groups, must also exist. This is the province of mental health, but there must be collaboration to reach those suffering from psychological and emotional difficulties, particularly those who are depressed or have suicidal thoughts. Improving communications within schools and between schools and relevant agencies can help rely information about threats, suspicious behavior, or incidents involving students or others who may be connected to schools in one form or another.

The presence of increased school security can be useful in deterrence and intervention efforts, yet they alone cannot guarantee a school setting free from violence (Learning Never Stops, 2012).

School shootings continue to occupy the nation's attention and concern when it comes to conceptualizing security. In reality, such events are extremely rare; other forms of violence that threaten the safety, health and well-being of our children and adolescents occur at a much more frequent rate and practices and protocols to address them need to be a part of any larger-scale attempt to make a school community more secure.

FINAL THOUGHTS

School disturbance has existed throughout the educational history of this country. Beginning with the earliest formal schooling, there have been acts of aggression, bullying, and violence against both students and school personnel. While definitions of school violence in earlier times essentially came down to acts of physical violence, it was recognized that taunting and other kinds of verbal and psychological abuse also fell into this category. Early schooling was the privilege of the upper class, and so a great deal of homogeneity existed in the classroom. As the country's mission to educate all citizens evolved, so did class differences and ethnic backgrounds of the students who received formal schooling.

As new immigrants come to America, a primary function of public schools continues to be to ready a diverse population to become full citizens through language acquisition, acculturation, career preparation, and smooth transitions to postsecondary options. While school security once was conceived as keeping our students physically safe on the school grounds and in the classrooms, the notion of emotional, psychological and social security has become a key element of the evolution of school safety planning. Many of students' fears about their safety emanate from the perceived and real threats that come once they leave the school building. Forming partnerships with neighborhoods and community groups that surround the school can lead to initiatives that enhance the school's security efforts. The "village" can raise a child only when it can ensure his or her safe passage to and from school, home, and other important institutions.

POINTS TO REMEMBER

- *School disturbances have existed throughout the entire educational history of the United States.*
- *Definitions of what constitutes school violence have evolved from purely physical definitions to those recognizing verbal violence and its effects, and expanded to consider exclusion, deliberate targeting of groups, and cyber victimization.*
- *Relationships between students' sense of connectedness, being valued, and belonging at school and their sense of security are inextricably linked.*
- *Schools can take actions to assess their environments and create cultures that cultivate socio-emotional health and well-being.*
- *Students who are exposed to school violence, especially if exposures are frequent and persist over time, are prone to mental health problems such as anger, depression, anxiety, and hypervigilance.*
- *There are tenuous links between diagnosed mental illness and school violence, although there is evidence that gun-related violence in which the perpetrator takes his or her own life is related to diagnosed conditions.*
- *Mental health needs of children and adolescents of school age are escalating and schools most often are the de facto providers of services, although few have the resources to do this effectively.*

Chapter 2

Understanding Variations of Violence
Defining "Safety" in the Schoolhouse

The term "school violence" tends to engender an image of a school shooting, with SWAT teams surrounding a school and hordes of terrified students fleeing the scene, often with hands on top of their heads. The media coverage of such incidents as the Columbine and Parkland shootings have been seared into the American brain, yet there are many other forms of school violence, often subtler and more submerged, that exist in contemporary American schools. This can range from the deliberate exclusion of certain groups from textbooks, policies, or social acceptance to outright acts of violence which can cause lasting harm, physically and emotionally.

DEFINITIONS OF VIOLENCE

The Merriam Webster Dictionary (n.d.) defines violence as "the use of physical force so as to injure, abuse, damage, or destroy; an instance of violent treatment or procedure; injury by or as if by distortion, infringement, or profanation; or intense, turbulent, or furious and often destructive action or force" (n.p.). All of these definitions make sense when considering violence in contemporary schools.

The World Health Organization (WHO) (2018) defined violence as "the intentional use of force or power against oneself, others, or a group or community" (n.p.). Their definition includes force that is threatened or actual, and that either results in harm or has a high likelihood of doing so. Harm, according to the WHO (2018) definition, can include "death, psychological injury, maldevelopment, or deprivation" (n.p.).

Some authors, such as Kraus (2005) have taken issue with this broad definition of violence. The WHO (2018) definition would consider an act violent even if the perpetrator was not able to accurately assess its full potential for harm. By inserting the notion of intentionality into their definition, Kraus (2005) argues, the World Health Organization "implicitly promulgates a volition model of human action" (p. 14). Kraus (2005) also raises cross-cultural questions, as in the example of teachers using force against their students to improve their academic performance, which would, under the WHO's (2018) definition, be violent behavior, even if it were a cultural norm in a particular society. These examples illustrate the difficult nature of defining violence.

Violence is generally categorized in three, broad ways to include self-directed violence, interpersonal violence, and acts of collective violence (Afzaal, 2012). Violent acts can be expressed through physical, emotional, psychological, or sexual means (Afzaal, 2012). In terms of school violence, self-directed and interpersonal are most common, but many would argue that there also are more subtle, political kinds of violence perpetrated by larger forces in our society.

Self-Directed Violence

Self-directed violence is comprised of suicidal behavior and self-injury (Hartford, Hsiao-ye, & Freeman, 2012). The first category includes completed suicide, suicidal ideation, and attempted suicide. Self-abuse, in contrast, includes acts such as cutting or causing other kinds of physical harm to oneself.

Collective Violence

Collective violence is that which is perpetrated by larger groups of people, governments, or states against individuals or specific, targeted groups (Klevens, 2011). In many instances, collective violence is committed to advance a particular social agenda; this category includes such actions as crimes of hate committed by organized groups, terrorist acts, and mob violence.

There also may be violence committed through political acts, such as war and related violent conflicts, state violence and similar acts carried out by larger groups (Klevens, 2011). Economic violence also exists and includes attacks by groups motivated by economic gain—such as attacks carried out with the purpose of disrupting economic activity, denying access to essential services, or creating economic imbalance among groups and individuals. Many argue that there are also types of violence that are endemic to society, such as poverty, oppressive government policies, or disparities in access to goods such as clean water, healthy food, or medical services (Klevens, 2011).

Non-physical

Violence includes those acts that result from a power relationship, including threats and neglect as well as intimidation of others (United Nations Educational, Scientific, and Cultural Organization, 2017). Such non-physical violence results in such experiences as psychological harm, deprivation and detrimental effects on human development. Violence may not always result in injury or death, but it does place a substantial burden on individuals, families, communities and health care systems globally (United Nations Educational, Scientific, and Cultural Organization, 2017). Many forms of violence against women, children and the elderly, for instance, can result in physical, psychological and social problems and costs. It is important to consider non-physical violence, as well as that which is physical, as its effects can be immediate, as well as latent, and can last for years after the original abuse (United Nations Educational, Scientific, and Cultural Organization, 2017).

Interpersonal Violence

Interpersonal violence is violence that occurs largely between family members and intimate partners, usually, though not exclusively, in the home (Butchart, Mikton, Dalhberg, & Krug, 2014). Community is expressed as violence between individuals who are unrelated, and who may or may not know each other, generally taking place outside the home. The former group includes forms of violence, such as battering one's partner, the abuse of children and the elderly, or sexual violence in an intimate relationship; while the latter includes youth violence, random acts of violence, sexual assault by strangers, and violence in institutional settings such as schools, workplaces, prisons and nursing homes (Butchart, Mikton, Dalhberg, & Krug, 2014).

Child Maltreatment

Child maltreatment affects children under eighteen years of age. It encompasses both neglect and outright abuse of many kinds, including all types of physical and/or emotional ill-treatment, neglect or sexual abuse, and commercial exploitation of or exploiting children in other ways (Pekarsky, 2018). Such violence against children can result in immediate or future harm to the child's health, survival, development, personal dignity, trust, or power. Exposure to intimate partner violence, such as seeing one's mother physically abused by one's father, often also is included in the definition of child maltreatment (Pekarsky, 2018).

There are no reliable global estimates for the rate of occurrence of child maltreatment because many countries, especially low- and middle-income countries, lack regular data collection of such statistics. Current estimates are widely divergent depending on the country and the method of research used; however, approximately 20 percent of women and 5–10 percent of men report being sexually abused as children, while 25–50 percent of all children report being physically abused (Abbasi, Saeidi, Khademi, Hoseini, Moghadam, 2015). Consequences of child maltreatment may include impaired lifelong physical and mental health, and social and occupational functioning, such as school, job, or relationship difficulties.

Youth Violence

As defined by the World Health Organization (2016), youth are between the ages of ten and twenty-nine years. Youth violence refers to violence occurring between or among young people and includes acts that span from bullying and physical fighting to sexual and physical assault, to homicide. Youth between the ages of ten and twenty-nine account for 43 percent of the total number of homicides each year and, for each fatality worldwide, another 20–40 youth are harmed seriously (WHO, 2016). Obviously, many youth already suffer the effects of child maltreatment and abuse mentioned previously.

Intimate Partner Violence or Domestic Violence

Intimate partner violence refers to actions committed in an intimate relationship that cause "physical, sexual or psychological harm, including physical aggression, sexual coercion, psychological abuse and controlling behaviours" (WHO, 2017, n.p.). Intimate partner and sexual violence can result in devastating "short- and long-term physical, mental, sexual and reproductive health problems" (WHO, 2017, n.p.) affecting not only victims, but also their children. Society bears the high costs of these acts, which run the gamut from fatal and non-fatal injuries, depression and post-traumatic stress disorder, unwanted pregnancies and sexually transmitted infections, including such diseases as HIV (Breiding, Basile, Smith, Black, & Mahendra, 2015).

Sexual Violence

Sexual violence includes "any sexual act, attempt to obtain a sexual act, unwanted sexual comments or advances, or acts to traffic, or otherwise directed, against a person's sexuality using coercion, by any person regardless of their relationship to the victim, in any setting, including but not limited to home and work" (Krug, Mercy, Dahlberg, & Zwi, 2002, p. 149). It includes rape, which is "defined as the physically forced or otherwise coerced penetration . . . of the vulva or anus with a penis, other body part or any object" (Krug, Mercy, Dahlberg, & Zwi, 2002, p. 149).

It is estimated that up to 11.5 percent of women reported experiencing sexual violence (Brieding, Smith, Basile, Walters, Chen & Merrick, 2014). Sexual violence has serious short- and long-term consequences on sexual, mental, physical, and reproductive health for victims and for their children, similar to those described in the section on intimate partner violence (Krug, Mercy, Dahlberg, & Merrick, 2002). If sexual violence occurs during childhood, it can lead to increased risks for smoking, drug and alcohol misuse, and risky sexual behaviors in adolescence and adulthood. It is also associated with perpetration of violence and being a victim of violence.

Targeted Violence

Targeted violence includes assassinations, attempted assassination and school shootings that take place in elementary, middle, high schools, or colleges and universities in the United States (Borum, 2015). Several studies have created a profile of those who engage in targeted violence (Dumitriu, 2013; Hickey, 2014). A major point from these research studies is that targeted violence does not just come on suddenly, when the perpetrator "snaps," but actually is the result of premeditated planning (Dumitriu, 2013; Hickey, 2014).

OVERVIEW OF SCHOOL VIOLENCE

School shootings such as Columbine High School in 1999 have traumatized this nation. In 2001, more than 50 percent of parents of K-12 students and 75 percent of high school students believed that a shooting could happen at their school; those numbers have skyrocketed with growing media and national attention to the shootings that followed (Juvonen, 2001). While incidents of school shootings still are very low, the perception is that they could occur anytime, anywhere. And other forms of school violence, as covered later in this chapter, continue to rise.

According to the Centers for Disease Control and Prevention, more commonly referred to as the CDC, (2016), school violence is defined as "youth violence that occurs on school property, on the way to or from school or school-sponsored events, during a school-sponsored activity" (p. 1). It most frequently involves behaviors such as physical assault, fighting, use of weapons, electronic aggression, bullying, or gang-related violence (Centers for Disease Control and Prevention, 2016).

While school-associated violent deaths are rare, less than 2.6 percent of youth homicides occur at school, there are troubling statistics that indicate the wider scope of school violence (Centers for Disease Control and Prevention, 2016). In 2013, for example, 12 percent of students ages 12–18 had gangs present in their schools; in 2015, 9–12th graders nationally reported that 8 percent had been in a physical fight on school property; almost 6 percent did not attend school one or more days due to safety concerns; 20 percent were bullied on school property and 15 percent electronically; 6 percent were threatened or injured by a weapon on school property at least once during the past year; and 4 percent carried a weapon on school property on one or more days (Centers for Disease Control and Prevention, 2016).

There are a number of factors that increase the risk of youth violence at school, but the mere presence of one of these factors doesn't mean that the violence will occur. These factors include association with delinquent peers, poor family functioning, low grades in school, poverty, substance abuse, prior history of violence, and mental health issues, with this factor gaining greater attention by the day (Juvonen, 2001).

Garabarino (1995) speaks to the risks inherent in toxic living environments, noting that the factors mentioned previously do not in and of themselves lead to violent behavior

> as the social environment becomes more toxic, it is the most vulnerable children who show the effects first, those who have accumulated the most developmental risk factors. . . . Such accumulation overwhelms the child—particularly when it occurs without a parallel accumulation of opportunity factors. Once overwhelmed, children are likely to fall prey to the socially toxic influences that surround them (p. 4).

Krauss (2005) points out that violence has always existed and it is a part of everyday life in America. Krauss (2005) reports figures, derived from parental reports, that in United States inner cities, 84 percent of first and second grade students had witnessed some form of community violence and 21 percent had been directly victimized; while fifth and sixth grade students' experiences rose to 90 and 35 percent respectively. The author points out that schools, in comparison, are relatively safe havens compared to these neighborhoods in which students live, yet schools, too, can be settings of violence.

Students aged eight to fifteen rank bullying as a greater problem in their lives than discrimination or racism (Juvonen, 2001). But bullying and more serious violence are too frequently intertwined. Childhood bullies are more likely to be involved in person-oriented crime in young adulthood and, additionally, a small percentage of youth simultaneously perceive themselves as the targets of bullying while engaging in bullying themselves.

As the spate of school violence continues, schools scramble to implement programs to decrease school violence. Among these have been physical surveillance methods, school resource officers and other personnel on campus, counseling for at-risk individuals, profiling potentially violent individuals, conflict mediation and resolution programs to include peer mediation, instructional programs created to address the precursors of violence, and school policies for prevention and punishment of incidents of violence (Juvonen, 2001).

MICROAGGRESSIONS

Although one tends to think of larger forms of violence as the major problem facing schools today, microaggressions are a root cause of violent acts (Sue, 2010; Runyowa, 2015). Microaggressions are defined as insults, remarks, offhand comments, or other non-verbal cues that suggest negative or hateful attitudes toward targeted, and often marginalized, populations (Sue, 2010). Sue (2010) writes that often,

> these hidden messages may invalidate the group identity, or experiential reality of target persons, demean them on a personal or group level, communicate they are lesser human beings, suggest they do not belong with the majority group, threaten and intimidate, or relegate them to inferior status and treatment (p. 1).

Microaggressions come in many forms and can be heard—whether they were intentionally or unintentionally aimed at target students—in our schools on a daily basis (Runyowa, 2015). They might be racial in nature, or gender-based, such as women and girls being subjected to comments about their bodies or their status as a sex object. They also may be related to sexual orientation, such as saying that something that is not liked or not seen to be of value as being "so gay." They also could be representative of social class bias, such as "trailer trash," or religious intolerance, such as "Don't try to Jew me down" (Sue, 2010).

Microaggressions can take place in both face-to-face and online venues and typically take place on a smaller scale (Sue, 2010). When they take place over time and are not confronted by those in power or by education aimed at raising awareness of how deeply ingrained some of these biases are in our culture, they can raise the targets' levels of frustration, hurt and anger (Runyowa, 2015).

BULLYING

While bullying may take on slightly different meanings dependent upon the lens from which it is viewed, Bridging Refugee Youth and Child Services [BRYCS] (n.d.) defines it as a unique form of aggressive behavior that is intentional, harmful, repetitive in nature, and in which there is an imbalance of power (either psychological or physical) between the aggressor and victim. . . . The way cultures define "bullying" can vary. While it always involves the abuse of power and harm to another individual, it takes different forms in societies based on culture (p. 1).

Each type of violence, then, takes this broad definition and adds the specifics to focus the attention on the issue at hand.

XENOPHOBIC VIOLENCE

There is very little research on bullying in multicultural contexts and few conclusions about factors such as race, ethnicity, and religion individually, or in combination; however, "there is a good deal of overlap between bullying and bias incidents, harassment, and hate crimes in school, which typically involve race, ethnicity, or other identity factors" (BRYCS, n.d., p. 1). School-aged immigrant youth face a number of challenges as part of the immigration and assimilation process that may place them in a more susceptible position to bullying victimization in and out of school (Maynard, Vaughn, Salas-Wright, & Vaughn, 2016).

One study examined whether immigrant youth were more likely than native-born youth to experience bullying victimization, whether there are differences in bullying victimization by gender, and to identify any "correlates of bullying victimization among immigrant youth" (Maynard et al., 2016). Immigrant youth were significantly more likely to experience one or more forms of bullying than their U.S.-born counterparts, even after controlling for a number of demographic variables (Maynard et al., 2016).

The Maynard et al. (2015) findings are similar to other studies examining immigrant youth and bullying victimization in other countries. Students of color, Jewish and Muslim students, and those from refugee camps were more likely to experience bullying related to religious or racial factors (BRYCS, n.d.). Bullying based on racial/ethnic differences also was found, and this finding is particularly important given recent research on the relationship between discrimination and acculturation with mental health and maladjustment among minority populations.

Not all prior research found that immigrant youth were more likely to be bullied than native-born youth (Maynard et al., 2016). Variation in findings could be contextually and culturally dependent; cultural differences in countries where studies took place, in terms of their acceptance and treatment of immigrants and the culture of immigrants coming to those countries, could explain differences in findings. Certain immigrant groups may be more at risk in specific host countries due to the extent of similarities and differences in culture, language, physical characteristics, attitudes, and behavior (Maynard et al., 2016).

The researchers had hypothesized that immigrant youth who reported bullying victimization would be more likely to indicate lower levels of well-being across measures related to health and intra- and interpersonal factors, and higher levels of substance use than immigrants who were not victimized, and this hypothesis was borne out. With the exception of three indicators, immigrants who experienced bullying victimization fared worse than their non-bullied immigrant counterparts; for example, being overweight increased an immigrant's chances of being bullied, while being more similar to the majority culture decreased bullying incidences (Maynard et al., 2016).

The relationship between bullying and health and well-being is a difficult one to tease out, as the authors note, since cause and effect are not immediately identifiable. Immigrant and refugee students can be the perpetrators of bullying, often in an attempt to affiliate or belong to a group (BRYCS, n.d.). Many refugee students have had to develop strong survival skills and may attack or fight back in the face of perceived threats. These perceived threats may be typical interactions or "horsing around" for American students, yet they can be interpreted differently by those who have had to be hypervigilant in dangerous settings.

Demographics of a school can affect the prevalence of bullying involving these populations (Smokowski, Cotter, Robertson, & Guo, 2013). The greater the ethnic diversity in the school, the less chance that immigrant/refugee students feel vulnerable, or like "outsiders," resulting in a greater balance of power among disparate groups. A school climate in which there is knowledge about different members of the community, where diversity is discussed and celebrated, and where racism, anti-immigrant sentiment, or religious or political tensions are directly confronted is more likely to help with immigrant integration and reduce incidences of bullying and conflict (American Psychological Association [APA], 2018a).

SUICIDE AMONG THE SCHOOL-AGE POPULATION

Korte (2017) wrote on the rising rates of youth suicide, citing a double in the number of patients aged five to seventeen who have been hospitalized for suicidal thoughts or actions in the period from 2007 to 2015. The author quotes medical staff who believe that as school systems are becoming more challenging, and bullying and weapons more common, many students are driven to consider suicide as a solution to their problems. Another consideration is the "seasonality" of suicide; that is, school-aged students attempt the act in the fall and spring, while adults are more apt to attempt suicide during the summer months (Korte, 2017).

While society is primed to believe that suicide is not an act performed by children, recent statistics prove otherwise. A new report shows that, for the first time, suicide rates for U.S. middle school students have surpassed the rate of death by car crashes (McBride, 2016). The suicide rate among youngsters has been steadily rising, and doubled in the United States between 2007 to 2014, with 425 young people ten to fourteen years of age dying by suicide (McBride, 2016).

An increase in suicides among school children also includes more dramatic ways of harming themselves such as hanging and suffocation, as well as suicidal thoughts that may not be acted upon, or may be thwarted (Rock, 2018). Today's youth have access to much more information about how to harm themselves (Korte, 2017; Rock, 2018). The internet and other media may not only be increasing the rate of cyberbullying, which is known to be linked to depression and suicidal behaviors in young people but may be the repository of graphic information about ways to end one's life (Korte, 2017). Simply viewing bullying behavior without necessarily participating in it leaves students feeling more helpless and less connected to school and family.

The use of social media can also convey information about suicide in more intimate ways. This may be a reason for "cluster suicides" that are becoming increasingly familiar in our schools. Kutner (2016) speaks of student suicide as "contagious," chronicling the suicides in El Paso County, Colorado and its neighboring county, Douglas. At those schools, students had ended their lives through gunshot, hangings, and drug overdoses, as well as choking deaths that parents believed were accidental, although newer waves of death by choking are becoming increasingly more common (Kutner, 2016).

Although sociologists have long written that individuals who have bonds with others are less likely to commit suicide or other acts of violence, Kutner (2016) finds this logic to be turned on its head by the suicide contagion. As early as 1990, it was confirmed that suicide could be contagious and transmitted between individuals; adolescents aged fifteen to nineteen were two to four times more likely to be susceptible to this than any other age group (Kutner, 2016). Cluster suicides make up between 1 to 5 percent of total suicides (Kutner, 2016). These may be among the more preventable suicides but, if carried out, they wreak the most havoc on schools and communities. More than three times as many teens commit suicide as occurred in the 1950s in this country (Kutner, 2016).

In the early 1970s it was believed that one suicide generally had a profound impact on six people and was limited mostly to close family members (Kutner, 2016). As of today, the number is pegged at 135, with a third experiencing severe life disruption (Kutner, 2016). Those who know a suicide victim are almost twice as likely to develop suicidal thoughts as is someone in the general public. With social media exploding, the chances are that these rates will increase (Kutner, 2016).

Social media continue to be a growing problem, Kutner (2016) writes, because Instagram pages can memorialize dead students in ways that appear to glamorize death or promote the allure of suicide as a way to solve problems and find peace. Impressionable students may be influenced by the death of someone they have absolutely no real-life connection with. With many accounts at over a thousand followers, it is not hard to see the power of media accounts to exacerbate this social problem (Kutner, 2016).

The Silicon Valley Suicides raised similarly troubling questions about why so many bright, well-liked, successful students, who seemingly had everything one could want, had committed suicide in Palo Alto. Luthar (as cited in Rosin, 2015), a psychiatric researcher who began her career studying the behaviors of youth to discover if misbehavior correlated more with poverty or adolescence as a developmental stage. Beginning her studies with an inner-city school where 86 percent of the population was on free and reduced lunch, she needed a comparative site, so she chose a school that was extremely affluent (Rosin, 2015). Little did she expect to find that students at the affluent school used drugs and alcohol at significantly higher rates and that they had higher rates of serious anxiety and depression (Luthar, 2003). This began her long career looking at the vulnerabilities of students in a "culture of affluence" (Luthar, 2003).

A largely unrecognized "at risk" group, the most affluent youth are usually overlooked because they have material items, good grades, and seemingly endless future possibilities; the truth, as Luthar (2003) found, is that many are not handling adolescence successfully. Such was the case in Palo Alto, where the pressure to excel in everything created enormous psychological pressures, often derived from parental expectations from whom students felt remarkably isolated (Rosin, 2015). These pressures and expectations, often having little goodness of fit for the adolescents as individuals, must be added to the commonly circulated lists of indicators of suicide mentioned below.

Risk Factors

In Colorado, after the wave of suicides, the Colorado Child Fatality Prevention System investigated and discovered common risk factors among the victims to include family arguments, physical or emotional abuse, breaking up with a boyfriend or girlfriend, and a number of students who were children of parents serving in the military, who are at higher risk for suicide than the general public (Kutner, 2016). If young people do not have the coping skills to get through stressful times, a sequence of smaller events, such as failing a test, when coupled with larger ones, may set off a chain reaction that moves him or her from thinking about suicide to attempting it.

There are common warning signs that often go unnoticed or unreported (Korte, 2017). These should not be ignored and include talking to others or posting on social media a range of emotions—from wanting to die, feeling hopeless or trapped, or being a burden to others (American Foundation for Suicide Prevention, 2018). There also may be an accumulation of information and/or instrumentation such as firearms, medication or online resources that could lead to implementation. Those considering suicide may give away their possessions or call or visit others to say goodbye. They may also move away from a period of depression or agitation to calm and cheerfulness (American Foundation for Suicide Prevention, 2018).

Sexual Violence

Bates (2017) chronicles the rising concern in the United Kingdom related to the issue of sexual violence in schools, citing the story of an elementary student named Emily. Emily reported being physically assaulted by a male classmate, but her school administration did little to help her. Bates (2017) writes that when "Emily tried to speak to the school about the incident, they quickly dismissed it as 'a misunderstanding', telling her: 'Everyone's happy now.' But Emily was far from happy" (p. 1). Eventually, Emily explained to her parents that the boy had asked for oral sex and other things; yet, she did not tell because she believed she might have been pregnant and did not want her parents to be angry (Bates, 2017).

Emily's parents reached out to the school and many others for help; however, they were met with resistance at every turn. While her parents were appalled by the handling of her case, they did not completely blame the school administration, citing the lack of protocol laid out for school personnel to follow (Bates, 2017). Emily's case is similar, unfortunately, to others taking place globally, including in United States schools; her story is just one among many of sexual violence in schools, where confusion and inconsistency in the treatment of victims and survivors are commonplace.

Bullying and school gun violence may be receiving the bulk of the media attention these days, but sexual harassment in school, including such things as vicious rumor spreading, groping girls or calling boys a homophobic slur also constitutes an act of sexual harassment (Gordon, 2014). In any given school year, according to a 2014 report, 585 of seventh through twelfth graders experience some form of sexual harassment (Gordon, 2014). Girls are more likely to experience all forms of harassment, except for the pejorative uses of terms bashing the LGBTQ community (Gordon, 2014).

In the 2010–11 school year, 13 percent of all American school girls reported that they had been touched or groped in unwanted ways and 4 percent had been forced against their will to perform sexual acts (Gordon, 2014). Girls who were very well developed physically or deemed to be "very pretty" were the most likely targets, followed by boys who were not very masculine, girls who were not very attractive, and overweight children regardless of sexual orientation; good-looking boys were considered to be the least at risk of sexual harassment or attack (Gordon, 2014).

Other shocking statistics related to school sexual harassment include that one in twenty sexually harassed girls switches schools each year due to the abuse (Gordon, 2014). These upheavals force disruptions in girls' education as well as their social lives (Hill & Kearl, 2011). The AAUP study of school harassment cites the conventional wisdom that boys who sexually tease girls usually do so because they like the girl and want to get her attention; however, only 4 percent of boys who took part in the study did so because they wanted a date (Hill & Kearl, 2011).

Most did not see their behavior as "a big deal," denoting the vast difference between their interpretation and that of their victims. Victims reported staying home from school and having trouble sleeping because of their perpetrators' acts; most felt isolated and alone (Hill & Kearl, 2011). Gordon (2014) found that sixth grade boys who were bullies were five times as likely to engage in sexually harassing behaviors at school later. If they engaged in using gay slurs while in sixth grade, they were one and a half times more likely to be sexual harassers in high school (Gordon, 2014). In order to demonstrate that they were not gay themselves, such bullies expressed their "manhood" by taunting others.

Twenty percent of high school girls report being sexually assaulted by a peer; this goes beyond verbal taunting or rumor starting and is defined by actual sexual contact that is unwanted by the recipient (Gordon, 2014). Among these assaults were unwanted touching, kissing or hugging, and more serious violations. Twelve percent of the respondents said that they had been raped by a peer, while the 2013 Youth Risk Behavior Survey found that 10.5 percent of high school girls and 4.2%of boys reported peer rape (Gordon, 2014).

A study funded by the National Institute of Justice found that nearly 20% of both boys and girls reported being victims of sexual abuse in their intimate relationships (Crary, 2014). Dating abuse is one of the few incidents of sexual violence reported at equal levels by both sexes and the same study found that one in eight teenagers admitted to sexually abusing someone they had dated (Crary, 2014).

Interestingly, there were higher incidences of violent behavior and threats from twelve to fourteen-year-old girls, while boys became the more prevalent perpetrators as they got older. A shocking 60% of high school boys believe that it is acceptable to force sex upon girls under certain circumstances; for example, some felt that it was all right for a boy to force a girl to have sex "if they're in love" (Crary, 2014, n.p.).

Students who have been forced into sex are not forthcoming, with about only half saying that they told another person about it and it is even less likely that they report rape or sexual abuse to authorities (Crary, 2014). A tally of 4,200 sexual assaults in schools (600 rapes) in the 2009–2010 school year alone were reported, yet half of these were never reported to law enforcement (Crary, 2014). This is evidence against the twenty-three school districts currently facing Title IX sexual violation investigations due to mandated sexual assault reporting by any school that receives federal funding. This includes promptly conducting investigations, protecting victims and ensuring their safety.

HOMOPHOBIC VIOLENCE

Seven years ago a spate of suicides triggered widespread discussion about the extremely high rate of bullying of queer and transgender students; however, a new study by McKay, Misra, & Lindquest, (2017) claims the prevalence of anti-LGBTQ+ harassment and violence has risen considerably higher since 2000 after collecting and analyzing twenty years' worth of data.

The 2017 report is unprecedented in its scope (McKay et al., 2017). While it might appear that today's youth are more welcoming and accepting of the LGBTQ+ community, RTI's analysis came to the conclusion that the widespread targeting of this population has "not improved since the 1990s" (McKay et al., 2017). In fact, some forms of victimization actually appear to have grown worse among the youth population and these acts can have serious, lifelong impacts on the physical and behavioral health of LGBTQ+ youth and adults (McKay et al., 2017).

Across the studies reviewed, which included a combined sample of 73,000 LGBTQ+ youth, the rates of school bullying have reached unparalleled highs (McKay et al., 2017). Given thirty-five years of data, they concluded that LGBTQ+ students are two to three times more likely to be victimized at school than their peers (Lang, 2018). Several studies confirmed that LGBTQ+ high school students were three times more likely to be bullied than their straight classmates; with 71% of LGBTQ+ experiencing having the word "gay" used against them in a pejorative way, making 91% of them feel distressed at school (Liu, 2016; Ford, 2014).

The Teens, Health, and Technology Survey, conducted in 2014, found that 81 percent of transsexual youth are sexually harassed in school, as are

72 percent of lesbian students, while sixty-six percent of gay and bisexual teens report facing sexual harassment from their peers (Lang, 2018). By the end of middle school, 22 percent of trans students report being harassed due to their gender identity, and 19 percent because of their sexual orientation (Lang, 2018).

Viral stories of trans people tend to convey the impression things are improving in society. A transgender student in Santa Barbara, California, for example, was voted prom queen at Santa Barbara High School, with similar instances in states like New York, Florida, and North Carolina (Lang, 2018). But these feel-good stories are an amplification of success stories, with much less emphasis on school environments that are deemed too dangerous for LGBTQ+ student populations to exist comfortably on a day-to-day basis (Lang, 2018).

The evidence on the subject is overwhelming. The National School Climate Survey (Kosciw, Greytak, Giga, Villenas, & Danischewski, 2015) found that 55 percent of LGBTQ+ youth felt "unsafe" in schools in the past year because of concerns about their sexual orientation, and 75 percent of trans students did not feel comfortable attending class due to their status (Kosciw et al., 2015). LGBTQ+ students are 91% more likely to be bullied or harassed than their peers, the latest study showed, and three times more likely to be sexually assaulted (Kosciw et al., 2015).

For gender non-conforming students who begin secondary school with an established sense of gender identity, classmates were frequently the tormentors and high school violence was, sadly, commonplace (Wyss, 2004). Enduring this violence was extremely detrimental to the informants' emotional, physical and mental health; shame, low self-esteem, and anger ate at their psyches (Wyss, 2004). While many tried to escape being targeted, others dropped out or fought back, often with negative outcomes, and students often felt that there was no protection for them (Wyss, 2004).

Only twenty-eight states have laws on the books that explicitly provide nondiscrimination protections for LGBTQ+ people in public accommodations, including schools (Wyss, 2004). Of the teachers interviewed, 50 percent admitted that they had done absolutely nothing throughout their entire careers as educators to support their school's LGBTQ+ population, while not even a third had received any kind of professional developmental training on topics related to sexual orientation or gender identity (Wyss, 2004). School climate toward the LGBTQ+ students is less affirming in the South and in rural areas (Wyss, 2004).

Title IX of the Education Amendments of 1972—which, as of 2014, enumerates equal protections for trans students in schools—exists, but schools are often scared of doing the right thing and many times do not have clear policies nor adequate training for their staff (U.S. Department of Education,

Office for Civil Rights, 2015). In states in which there is strong political opposition to LGBTQ+ rights, schools and their personnel may be intimidated by threats of law suits (U.S. Department of Education, Office for Civil Rights, 2015).

VIOLENCE AGAINST TEACHERS

Any comprehensive examination of school violence must include violence directed at teachers. Focusing solely on student victimization to the exclusion of teacher victimization results in an inadequate representation of safety issues, which makes it more difficult to formulate effective solutions. Students are not always the perpetrators of violence against teachers. There also are documented incidents of adult-on-adult incidents—including parents and peers. Interestingly, physical attacks were more likely to come from a parent as opposed to a student.

The American Psychological Association (APA) published a report in which 80 percent of teachers surveyed reported that they had been victimized at school at least once in the current school year or prior year (Walker, 2013a). Violence against teachers has become a national crisis; however, this issue has taken a back seat to other forms of school violence in terms of media reporting and scholarship, creating a deficiency that has serious implications for school safety, the teaching profession and student learning (Espelage et al. 2013).

A rare national study derived its findings from a 2011 survey that solicited anonymous responses from almost 3,000 K-12 teachers in forty-eight states and revealed that about half reported being victimized through various types of harassment (Espelage et al., 2013). Approximately one-quarter of these teachers experienced physical attacks, while others reported property offenses, including theft and damage to property (Espelage et al., 2013).

Harassment was defined as activities ranging from obscene gestures, verbal threats, and intimidation to making obscene remarks (Espelage et al., 2013). Teachers reported physical violence that included objects being thrown at them and being physically attacked, while the most severe and rarest cases were physical attacks requiring outside medical attention (Espelage et al., 2013).

Teachers who are victimized once are more likely to be so again; yet it is not clear why this is true (Walker, 2013a). A student who harasses or threatens may be more likely to come from a family who is inclined to victimize the teacher in some way as well. There also may be teachers who court violence against them by their own attitude and/or behaviors (Walker, 2013a). Teachers in certain situations may not adequately be supported by the administration and consequently are at greater risk for other episodes (Espelage et al., 2013).

Teachers who experience school violence are more likely to leave the school or the profession, which results in lost wages, lost instructional time, negative publicity for the school, and a negative impact on student learning (Walker, 2013a). Teachers cannot perform their job effectively if they feel threatened (Espelage et al., 2013).

Future educators and administrators must be aware of the connection between positive school climate and lack of aggressive or violent behavior, as research connections are quite clear (Steffgen, Recchia, & Viechtbauer, 2013; Acosta et al., 2018). Strong leadership by the administration is needed to create a positive learning climate. Staff and students must understand the entire ecology of the school and the community and the essential nature of developing positive relationships (Acosta et al., 2018).

In this era of school budget cutbacks, many states are finding it difficult to find money for additional resources for teacher support (Long, 2012). Class sizes are getting larger and teachers are receiving less support, not more, both of which makes it more difficult to establish close relationships.

According to the Workplace Bullying Survey from June 2017, 19 percent of Americans believe they have been targeted, while another 19 percent say they have witnessed it (Workplace Bullying Institute, 2018). This translates into approximately 60.4 million individuals (Workplace Bullying Institute, 2018). Specific to the field of education, twenty-five percent of employees in mid-sized school districts reported incidences of bullying (Long, 2012).

An illustration of workplace bullying comes from Long (2012), who shared the story of a teacher from Augusta, Maine, whose experience so traumatized her, that even after the fact, she refused to use her real name as she was afraid of the repercussions.

> I am sufficiently frightened enough by my former employers to fear that maybe they could still hurt me," she says. "I need to get a new job but won't be able to do so if I am unable to receive even one recommendation from an administrator. I know it and so do they (as cited in Long, 2012, p. 1).

The educator refused both a grade and building transfer and shortly thereafter her performance, student test scores, family interactions, and relationships with colleagues came under scrutiny (Long, 2012). The administration interviewed each student in her class and when the educator questioned the students they told her "they were instructed not to tell" (Long, 2012, p. 2).

Administrators said that she did not sufficiently use technology and criticized her for utilizing a literacy mentor. The educator was required to turn in her lesson plans for review a week in advance and she was put on a behavior modification plan (Long, 2012). Her peers believed she was being targeted, her health began to suffer, and eventually she left her job.

According to Dr. Matt Spencer, "the bully steals the dignity, self-esteem, confidence, joy, happiness, and quality of life of the targeted victim." And when an educator is the target for violence, it is a great "injustice" because the bully deprives students of a caring adult who is crucial to their education (as cited in Long, 2012, p. 3).

FINAL THOUGHTS

Various forms of violence exist daily in American schools, and schools around the world. While media have recently turned their attention to gun violence in our nation's schools, there are many other kinds of violence that affect student and staff's safety, feelings of security, and ability to learn in an environment that is conducive to building community and academic achievement. Certain groups of students appear more likely to be targets of school violence and teachers and other school personnel themselves are not immune to attacks. Among these are girls, students of color, immigrant and refugee students, and those in the LGBTQ community.

It is generally accepted that strong school leadership is necessary to create a culture in which violence is not tolerated and all constituents of the school community are welcomed and respected. It also is clear that more must be done in higher education institutions as they prepare pre-service teachers and administrators to create such school cultures.

Schools need clear protocols for dealing with violence and more professional development, conducted with openness and honesty in the face of difficult and highly sensitive topics, must be provided in an ongoing fashion. With these steps, all students will be able to learn and thrive in their schools, rather than merely focus on surviving in dangerous terrain.

POINTS TO REMEMBER

- *There are various kinds of violence that can be perpetrated within contemporary American schools. Violence can be directed against individuals, groups, or self.*
- *Bullying, whether in school, outside of school, or cyberspace, is prevalent in contemporary schools. Bullying occurs when there is a perceived imbalance of power.*
- *Violence against girls is more common than against boys, unless those boys act in ways deemed "unmasculine."*

- *Large numbers of students from the LGBTQ+ community report being verbally or physically assaulted in school and do not feel safe in their school community.*
- *Groups of students perceived as "the other"—such as refugee, immigrant, or minority students—are at greater risk for school violence.*
- *Teachers and other school personnel also are at risk for violence, including assaults by students, other staff, administrators, or parents.*
- *It takes strong school leadership to establish a school culture in which violence is not tolerated and all constituents feel welcome and respected.*

Chapter 3

Crisis in the Classroom

The Mental Health Concerns of Children and Adolescents

The overall concept behind safe schools asserts that if children experience safety and happiness while in their daily school settings, they are more likely to reach their full potential, academically and psychologically (Weare & Gray, 2003). Students in healthy school environments develop and display self-confidence and self-esteem in high levels and their emotional health and well-being are enhanced (Duckett, Kagan, & Sixsmith, 2010). These positive qualities in students are linked to supportive relationships with their peers and teachers; in such settings, students report feeling that they are valued and respected members of the school community (Duckett et al., 2010).

Closely connected to safety in the schoolhouse is the state of contemporary students' mental health. When reviewing the cases of school shootings, bullying, suicides and other acts of violence within the school community, one is struck by the prevalence of mental health problems among the perpetrators. The issues range from low self-esteem, depression, and anxiety to suicidal ideation, narcissism, and psychopathology.

One in five individuals in this country is believed to have a diagnosable mental illness (Bekiempis, 2014). It is important to note that the majority of individuals with a mental illness do not commit violent actions; in fact, it is estimated that only a scant 4 percent of violence against others is committed by those who have been diagnosed (U.S. Department of Health & Human Services: Mental Health, 2017). Those with mental illness are more likely to be victims of crime than perpetrators; however, there are particular mental health issues—schizophrenia, major mood disorders, severe depression and bipolar disorder—that raise the risk of violent behavior (U.S. Department of Health & Human Services: Mental Health, 2017). Mental illness also increases the risk of suicide, or violence against the self. Alcohol and drug use and abuse also contribute to an increased risk in violence toward oneself (Safe and Sound Schools, 2016).

Historically, modern schools have been the de facto provider of mental health services, with more than 75 percent of children who received such services accessing them in schools; for many, this was their only avenue to mental health support (Adelman & Taylor, 2010). Over the last sixty years, American schools have devoted substantial time, money, services and thought as to how to best meet this need (Adelman & Taylor, 2010). Out of this concern arose the full-service in-school and school-linked services models that provide health, dental, mental health, family resources, after-school, and wellness programs, while other initiatives focused on youth development, community schools, and such curriculum as resiliency and assets-identification and building (Adelman & Taylor, 2010).

The authors also describe a gradual shift in thinking about these issues, moving from a mental illness model to that of mental health. This reflected a growing recognition that most students' mental health conditions are rooted in sociocultural and economic problems, not pathology, and that these can be countered by initiatives such as socioemotional curriculum and preventative interventions (Adelman & Taylor, 2010). A greater emphasis was placed on the devastating effects of child poverty on physical health, learning and mental wellness.

THE PREVALENCE OF THE PROBLEM

Anderson (2016) and Mahnken (2017) peg the prevalence of mental health disorders among children at approximately 20 percent of the population. Between the years of 2010 and 2015 there was a 50 percent increase in the number of hospitalizations due to children harming themselves, while children under the age of seventeen who were hospitalized with mood disorders rose by 68 percent from 1997 to 2011 (Page, 2017). In 2017, almost 80 percent of teachers in American schools reported noticing an increase in anxiety, panic attacks, and stress among their students, as well as a rise in the number of students who presented with eating disorders, depression, and self-harming behaviors (Page, 2017). Equally disturbing, the number of calls made to Childline, a national hotline, has doubled over five years' time, with 2016 bringing the "highest number of callers expressing suicidal thoughts" (Page, 2016, n.p.) In urban schools, upward of 50 percent of students have significant learning, behavioral, and/or emotional problems (Adelman & Taylor, 2010).

While the estimated numbers of children under the age of eighteen with mental, behavioral or emotional disorders translates to about 15 million across this country, estimates show that only about half receive either medication or psychological services and just 7.4 percent of adolescents say that they have visited a mental health professional over the past year (Mahnken, 2017).

As the number of those suffering from disorders rises (particularly those with ADHD, conduct disorders, depression, autism, and substance abuse), more and more families are without health insurance that will cover diagnosis and treatment. Schools, by default, have become the mental health system for too many children and families and these same children are far more likely to develop further issues, including criminal activity, substance abuse, and dropping out of school (Mahnken, 2017).

Schools themselves are ill-equipped to handle this epidemic. The National Association of School Psychologists, or NASP (2013b), recommends a ratio of one school psychologist for every 700 students, the ratio in American schools for the 2014–2015 school year was estimated to be about twice that; other educators in our schools are no less stressed, with a growing number of mandates and academic expectations and an increasingly fragile student population.

MENTAL HEALTH AND SCHOOL SAFETY

Teachers have a great deal of contact with their students, especially in the earlier grades; thus, they are often first to observe behaviors that may be indicators of mental health problems (Green, 2016). There are ten common mental health problems school-aged children are most likely to face with the most prevalent to include ongoing outbursts in class, aggressive behaviors, disengagement, antisocial behaviors, social isolation, or declining grades (Green, 2016). Mental health disorders can cause difficulties in learning, speaking, social interaction, behavior or emotional control—all of which are inextricably linked to academic, social, athletic, and emotional success (Green, 2016).

Attention-Deficit/Hyperactivity Disorder (ADHD). This disorder is marked by easy distraction, short attention spans, hyperactivity, excessive talking and constant interruptions of classroom process (Gaastra, Groen, Tucha, & Tucha, 2016). Both students and teachers suffer the consequences of this profile, as both learning and classroom management are under siege. Boys are far more likely to be diagnosed, although some have argued that, especially at the elementary level, with its preponderance of female teachers, some of these behaviors may be the result of a mismatch between teaching styles and boys' needs (Gaastra et al., 2016).

Anxiety. There are indications that this problem is growing. While anxiety may be displayed at school and in the classroom, it also wreaks havoc with the education of many children who may simply become too anxious to attend school at all or may suffer physical symptoms such as headaches or stomach troubles due to their condition (Moran, 2016).

Depression. Depression affects other students and most notably is evidenced by withdrawal or lack of interest in things a student once enjoyed (Faeq, 2016). Motivation and social interaction can be affected, although there are children and adolescents who are able to mask their pain very effectively. Depression over time can lead to suicidal thoughts or even actions. Educators and family should be on the alert for patterns of lowered grades, excessive tardiness, sleepiness, isolation and expressions of excessive sadness or lack of interest in the world (Faeq, 2016).

Autism Spectrum. A great variety of disorders fall along the autism spectrum. Students with these disorders often exhibit repetitive behavior. Their social skills may be impaired due to their inability to read social cues and nonverbal language (Young, Bonanno-Sotiropoulos, & Mumby, 2019). These disorders often are seen prior to school enrollment and range from severe to milder conditions, such as Asperger's Syndrome.

Oppositional Defiant Disorder (ODD). ODD is expressed most typically through negative and angry behaviors toward teachers and classmates. This hostile stance makes it difficult to manage classrooms due to hostile acting out and anger expressed toward others—everything from blaming others for one's mistakes to constant challenging of rules and social norms of classroom culture (Ross, 2017).

Conduct Disorder. Conduct disorder shares many traits of ODD. Challenging rules and arguing with others in the classroom are typical symptoms and students affected with conduct disorder often bully others while hiding their own low self-esteem in a cloak of tough actions (Frick, 2016). Conduct disorder may lead to absences from school, lying, and disciplinary problems.

Tourette Syndrome. Developing between the ages of three and nine, Tourette Syndrome affects approximately 1 percent of the population (Wadman, Glazebrook, Parkes, & Jackson, 2014). It is a neurological issue, that often presents as uncontrollable physical tics, and student efforts to control these distract them from being fully present in learning environments (Wadman et al., 2014). Other students may emit verbal tics, such as words or grunts, that they cannot suppress (Wadman et al., 2014). Obviously, such disorders interrupt the classroom and call unwanted attention to these children.

Eating Disorders. Eating disorders such as anorexia or bulimia trouble many young students, especially pre-adolescents and adolescents, and both boys and girls (Knightsmith, Treasure, & Schmidt, 2013). Eating disorders may be expressed as obsession with one's weight or food in general, unhealthy eating habits, and the inability to accurately gauge one's body image, so that the individual constantly views him or herself as "fat" (Knightsmith et al., 2013). There are certain categories of students—such as gymnasts, wrestlers, dancers or cheerleaders—who may be particularly prone to these concerns. Those with eating disorders may become very adept at hiding their conditions, and if left untreated, these conditions can lead to death (Knightsmith et al., 2013).

Post-traumatic stress disorder (PTSD). The medical profession has become more aware of its prevalence and causes during the last decade (Cohen, 2015). PTSD manifests when children have been through an experience or witnessed traumatic events (Cohen, 2015). There may be triggers that bring the child back to the actual event in flashbacks that evoke actual sensations similar to what had previously been experienced (Cohen, 2015).

Violent Students and Mental Health Profiles

Langman (2009, 2015), attempted to create psychological profiles of school shooters in the modern era based on three behavior types to include psychopathic, traumatized, and psychotic that provide fascinating glimpses into the inner workings of these students' minds.

Langman (2015) described psychopathic killers as arrogant, narcissistic, and entitled. They are driven to meet their own needs before others and, in fact, lack empathy for their victims (Langman, 2009). They are further described as holding many common traits such as "deceitfulness, 'impression management,' grandiosity, a strong drive for excitement, and a lack of empathy, guilt, and remorse" (Langman, 2015, p. 5). The author cites Eric Harris of the Columbine shootings as a classic example of a psychopathic killer.

Psychopaths have an exaggerated sense of their own importance and do not care if they hurt others; in fact, doing so may provide them with a rush of euphoria (Langman, 2015). Their social skills are highly honed to the point that they can lie with impunity and manage others' impressions of them in ways that cast them in a favorable light and hide their true ambitions. Psychopaths can be incredibly charismatic when they choose to do so, making them capable of high levels of deceit (Langman, 2009).

Psychopaths have little regard for social norms, values, or ethics; they dismiss the law, as they feel that they embody the law themselves (Langman, 2015). This attitude gives them a particular dislike for anyone in positions of authority and, as they do not feel fear, they are capable of being calm in situations that rattle typical individuals (Langman, 2015). Psychopaths avoid taking responsibility for their actions and tend to blame their victims for what has befallen them. Punishment evokes feelings of being wronged, as though an injustice was being meted out against them. Their narcissistic personalities lead them to believe that they are entitled to act as they see fit (Langman, 2009).

Psychopaths are extremely vulnerable to anything that they feel is a slight or a put down; thus, they are hypersensitive and may act out against any situation in which they are not in control (Langman, 2015). Their inflated self-images are prone to seeing such slights when there are none, and they feel justified in their actions if they perceive that a girlfriend, teacher, parent, or others have rejected or frustrated them (Langman 2009, 2015).

Psychopaths exhibit behavioral variations such as explosiveness, erupting in fury when they perceive that they have been slighted or disrespected, and becoming tyrannical and finding particular pleasure in ultimate power over their victims (Langman, 2015). Both qualities exist in psychopaths to some extent, such as Eric Harris, who both was known to explode over small issues and appeared to enjoy mocking the frightened students whom he eventually shot, according to those who survived the massacre (Langman, 2015).

Psychotic symptoms are found in several different diagnoses, including major depression and bipolar disorder and can range from chronic to episodic, narrowly problematic to widely debilitating (Rothschild, 2013). The school shooters that Langman (2015) discusses, however, appear to have suffered from schizophrenia or schizotypal personality disorder.

Schizophrenia, the more severe of the two conditions, results in the experience of hallucinations or delusions; schizophrenic individuals "struggle socially, are often desperately lonely, and are prone to depression" (p. 25). While those with schizotypal personality disorders are often socially impaired and viewed as "odd" in appearance, behavior or speech, they do not tend to have hallucinations and delusions—merely strange or atypical beliefs or ideas (Langman, 2015; Rothschild, 2013).

Those living with schizophrenia often speak of not trusting their own brains, of being exhausted from trying to separate what is real from what is delusional (Rothschild, 2013). Their very personalities are disturbed, in that they may not even know whether they are human or not. West Paducah, Kentucky school shooter, Michael Carneal, once noted, "I think I am an alien, but I'm not sure" (Langman, 2015, p. 34). Those who interviewed him post-rampage noted that in the weeks leading up to the shooting of a group of popular students, Carneal had been depressed and paranoid, believing that others were turning against him and hearing voices telling him to stand up for himself (Langman, 2015).

Langman (2009, 2015) reports that while most school shooters did not have terrible childhoods, there is a subpopulation who underwent not only abusive childhoods, but other traumatizing events. They are defined as traumatized shooters and most lived in substandard conditions, suffered childhood abuse and neglect, and experienced major loss and disruption within their families (Kiehl & Hoffman, 2011). Parents were lost to these children through death, divorce, brain damage, institutionalization, or incarceration, while others may have been physically present but were emotionally and psychologically absent due to their own mental illness or substance abuse

(Kiehl & Hoffman, 2011). Physical and sexual abuse were common; the children were traumatized by the chaos, violence, shame and terror they endured in their early years that eventually moved from emotions to uncontrollable rage (Kiehl & Hoffman, 2011).

The Causes of Mental Illness

The answer to what causes mental illness most likely lies both within the individual's biology and within the environment, the world in which someone lives and functions (Weir, 2012). External or environmental causes are extensive and can include chronic stressors, such as economic hardship or social struggles; poverty and other factors that cause dissatisfaction with the quality of one's life; trauma and adverse childhood experiences; exposure to toxins; problems within the family or with other important relationships; a history of childhood neglect or abuse (physical, sexual, emotional); substance abuse and risk-taking behaviors; parental instability, substance abuse, lack of employment, or mental illness; or any combination of these factors (Peterson, 2018a; Peterson, 2018b).

But while adversity in an individual's environment can be a cause or contributing factor to mental illness, the picture is far more complex as a combination of forces is at play in any situation. In order for someone to develop post-traumatic stress disorder (PTSD), for example, s/he must both experience a trauma, either personally or vicariously, *and* have a biological or genetic predisposition to developing PTSD (Peterson, 2018a). Without this necessary interplay of factors, all people exposed to any kind of trauma would automatically suffer from PTSD; as this is not the case, researchers are studying individuals who appear to thrive or have "post-traumatic growth" after such experiences (Chaisson, 2013).

CHILD TRAUMA AS A MAJOR CHILDHOOD MENTAL HEALTH ISSUE

One of the major issues that contemporary American schools confront is the fact that so many of their students, even the youngest, come to school having witnessed or experienced traumatic events. A traumatic event is one that is frightening, dangerous, or violent; it poses a threat to a child's life or bodily safety (de Bellis & Zisk, 2014). It is not a requirement that a child actually experiences the event firsthand for it to be traumatic; witnessing a traumatic event that harms another or even threatens the life or safety of a loved one can also be traumatic (De Bellis & Zisk, 2014). This is referred to as "vicarious" or "second hand" trauma. In younger children, there is an increased likelihood that being witness to such events will result in trauma since children's safety is inextricably linked to the perceived safety of those to whom they are attached (de Bellis & Zisk, 2014).

Experiencing a traumatic event may lead to an individual's undergoing powerful emotions, feelings of helplessness, anger, physical reactions, and other symptoms that may persist well into the future (de Bellis & Zisk, 2014). This can result in emotions such as terror or fear, disruptions in sleep patterns, or other outcomes such as heart palpitations, vomiting, or loss of bowel or bladder control as well as addictions to drugs or alcohol or self-harming behaviors (The National Child Traumatic Stress Network, n.d.b). Additional issues may include a loss of previously mastered skills, behavioral changes, lack of attachments, and risky behaviors (The National Child Traumatic Stress Network, n.d.b; Szalavitz, 2012). Children also may experience feelings of persistent fear, hypervigilance, and even guilt that they could not protect others from the traumatic event.

Types of Traumatic Events

There are a host of different events and experiences that can result in children's trauma to include

1. *Physical, sexual, or psychological abuse and neglect (including trafficking)*
2. *Natural and technological disasters or terrorism*
3. *Family or community violence*
4. *Sudden or violent loss of a loved one*
5. *Substance use disorder (personal or familial)*
6. *Refugee and war experiences (including torture)*
7. *Serious accidents or life-threatening illness*
8. *Military family-related stressors (e.g., deployment, parental loss or injury).* (The National Child Traumatic Stress Network, n.d.b, n.p.)

Simply experiencing the traumatic event is not necessarily the end of the trauma, as reminders of the event can crop up at any time, resulting in re-living the stress and emotions vividly (Szalavitz, 2012). These flashbacks and re-experiences can interfere with the child's daily life and ability to function and interact with others. Individuals are not always aware of potential triggers and cannot prepare themselves emotionally for their reactions (Szalavitz, 2012).

Without treatment, children and adolescents who have been exposed to traumatic events can suffer from damage to the brain or nervous system and are at higher risk for behaviors such as eating disorders, substance use, and other dangerous activities such as risky sexual behavior (The National Child Traumatic Stress Network, n.d.a; Szalavitz, 2012).

Child trauma survivors are more prone to die earlier, have long-term health issues, increased associations with child welfare and/or the juvenile justice system as well as a greater need for mental health services (The National Child Traumatic Stress Network, n.d.a; Szalavitz, 2012). Equally devastating, adult survivors of traumatic events may suffer from more depression than peers as well as "have difficulty in establishing fulfilling relationships and maintaining employment" (The National Child Traumatic Stress Network, n.d.a, n.p.).

The School Environment

Some authors look to the public schools themselves as a possible root cause of the recent epidemic of mental illness among children and adolescents (Strong, 2016; Gray, 2014). The CDC concluded that school connectedness plays a powerful role in preventing adolescent dysfunction, while the absence of such connection, the absence of meaningful relationships, and disengagement from the school community all put students at greater risk for violent actions (Strong, 2016).

Gray (2014) studied statistics on children's mental health through the calendar year and found that emergency psychiatric visits to the hospital were the lowest in July and August with the average number of visits for those two months registering at less than half the average of the full school months. June was also low in visit totals, as many schools are not in session or have limited days during that month. Gray (2014) postulates that the reason that May is the month highest in visits is that final exams, term papers, mandated curriculum completion all are due prior to the end of the year causing undue stress. There also has been speculation that the continued rise in the number of mental health issues among school children relates to the increased pressure of high-stakes testing and numerous assessments (von der Embse & Witmer, 2014).

A study of adverse childhood experiences, completed by The American Academy of Pediatrics (2014), concluded that incidences that range from single, acute events to those such as community violence or poverty that persist over time, can have an influence over the entire lifespan. Prolonged activation of the body's stress response system (toxic stress) may have a host of long-term effects at great cost to the individual and society (The American Academy of Pediatrics, 2014). The American Academy of Pediatrics (2014) classified childhood stress in three categories (1) positive, which helps guide growth; (2) tolerable, which causes no permanent damage; and (3) toxic, which can lead to long-term mental and physical health issues. How each child responds to stress is an interaction of personal qualities, perception of the stress, biology, and availability of protective factors.

RISK AND PROTECTIVE FACTORS THAT INFLUENCE MENTAL HEALTH AFTER A TRAUMATIC EVENT

In each individual case of a traumatic experience, there are a number of factors that influence the outcome to include the individual's make-up, past experience, and levels of school, family or community support as well as the severity of symptoms (Szalavitz, 2012, 2013). The National Child Traumatic Stress Network (n.d.b) describes five key variables that influence an individual's response to trauma.

- **Severity of the event.** How serious was the event? How badly was the child, or someone s/he loves, physically hurt? Did s/he or someone s/he loves need to go to the hospital? Were the police involved? Were children separated from their caregivers? Were they interviewed by a principal, police officer, or counselor? Did a friend or family member die?
- **Proximity to the event.** Was the child actually at the place where the event occurred? Did s/he see the event happen to someone else or was s/he a victim? Did the child watch the event on television? Did s/he hear a loved one talk about what happened?
- **Caregivers' reactions.** Did the child's family believe that he or she was telling the truth? Did caregivers take the child's reactions seriously? How did caregivers respond to the child's needs, and how did they cope with the event themselves?
- **Prior history of trauma.** Children continually exposed to traumatic events are more likely to develop traumatic stress reactions.
- **Family and community factors.** The culture, race, and ethnicity of children, their families, and their communities can be a protective factor, meaning that children and families have qualities and or resources that help buffer against the harmful effects of traumatic experiences and their aftermath. One of these protective factors can be the child's cultural identity. Culture often has a positive impact on how children, their families, and their communities respond, recover, and heal from a traumatic experience. However, experiences of racism and discrimination can increase a child's risk for traumatic stress symptoms (The National Child Traumatic Stress Network, n.d.b, n.p.).

There are myriad factors that can affect an individual's "chance of developing a mental and/or substance abuse disorder" (Substance Abuse and Mental Health Services Administration [SAMHSA], 2018, n.p.). Both risk and protective factors must be considered in the mental health equation. Risk factors precede and increase the chances of negative mental and emotional health outcomes and are influenced at the biological, family, cultural, community or psychological levels, while protective factors are just the opposite—variables that lower the risk of negative outcomes (SAMHSA, 2018).

In the cases of risk and protective factors, some characteristics are fixed while others may change over time, given an individual's life experiences and events (SAMHSA, 2018). Risk factors at the individual level include such things as predisposition to certain illnesses and additions, prenatal care, and early childhood experiences (SAMHSA, 2018). Individual protective factors could be social competence skills, internal locus of control, and positive self-esteem (SAMHSA, 2018).

SAMHSA (2018) posits a mental health model that takes into account that each individual's biological and psychological traits exist in many different contexts—family, community, school, and larger society. People do not exist in isolation; thus, educators and counselors must take a wholistic approach when determining the level of risk and protection each child or adolescent has when considered from individual, family, and community lenses (SAMHSA, 2018).

Within the individual sphere, such things as gender (female), early puberty, temperament, low self-esteem, anxiety, low-level depressive symptoms, and insecure attachment are among the risk factors (SAMHSA, 2018). Additional risk factors include social and communications skills, antisocial behavior, shyness, rebelliousness, head injury, and childhood exposure to neurotoxins (SAMHSA, 2018). As children progress toward adolescence, their attitudes toward drugs, early substance abuse, and favorable attitudes toward alcohol also put them at higher risk (SAMHSA, 2018).

At the family level, there are many potential risk factors. Among these are such variables as poor or inconsistent parenting, parental depression or mental illness, and abuse or maltreatment (SAMHSA, 2018). Divorce, parent-child conflict, marital conflict and spousal abuse, and parental substance abuse also weigh heavily (SAMHSA, 2018). Family dysfunction in general, including conflicts among extended family members, poor parental supervision, and unemployment can put children and adolescents in risky situations (SAMHSA, 2018).

School, neighborhood and community play powerful roles in shaping children's and adolescents' mental and emotional health. Poverty, community-level stress or traumatic events, and community violence can wreak havoc with health and well-being; thus, the same variables can be applied to the school level (SAMHSA, 2018).

Lack of connection in any of these venues, societal or community norms that discourage academic and vocational success, community tolerance of drug and alcohol use, and low commitment to postsecondary education also play roles. Negative peer associations, low self-esteem, loss of meaningful relationships, and school failure put youth at greater risk (SAMHSA, 2018).

However dismal risk factors may seem, there are buffers, in the form of protective factors. O'Connell, Boat, & Warner (2009) outline the many aspects of prosocial development that aid in positive mental and emotional health. At the individual level, positive physical development, emotional regulation, high self-esteem, and a sense of academic competence are important as are engagement and connections in two or more areas to include athletics, peers, school, religion, and culture (O'Connell et al., 2009).

At the familial level, protective factors include positive and supportive family relationships, an environment that gives children structure, limits, rules and predictability, clear expectations for their values and behaviors, and monitoring or supervision (O'Connell et al., 2009). A supportive school and community network provide other buffers such as positive norms, physical and psychological safety, a sense of belonging, mentors, opportunities for engagement, and chances to explore interests and passions (O'Connell et al., 2009).

Internal Protective Factors

Throughout studies of resilient individuals—those who have "overcome the odds"—there are common factors identified as "internal protective factors" that can serve as buffers even as children experience trauma or other stressful events (Henderson & Milstein, 2002). These factors, which can be fostered in schools and communities, reduce the risk posed by environmental hazards and promote positive mental and emotional health among youth.

Henderson and Milstein (2002) describe internal protective factors as sociability and the ability to act as a friend to others and form positive relationships. Using life skills, making good decisions, having impulse control, assertiveness and good problem-solving skills are also hallmarks (Henderson & Milstein, 2002). An internal locus of control, flexibility, self-motivation and a sense of personal competence also protect children and adolescents, as to feelings of self-worth and self-confidence, a desire to help others, and a personal faith or spiritual belief in something larger than the self (Reinemann & Ellison, 2008).

Werner (1992), Garmezy, Masten, & Tellegen (1984), and Rutter (1987) describe their own list of what they call critical developmental personality factors. These include an active, evocative approach to problem solving, enabling the individual to negotiate an array of emotionally hazardous experiences, and an optimistic view of one's experiences, even in the midst of suffering (Werner, 1992; Garmezy et al., 1984; Rutter, 1987).

Other personality factors are the ability to maintain a positive vision of a meaningful life as well as the ability to attract others and gain their positive attentions and mentoring (Garmezy et al., 1984). Other buffering traits are the ability to be alert, autonomy, a tendency to seek out novel experiences, and a proactive perspective (Werner, 1992).

Rutter (1987) wrote of the "four protective processes" (p. 1) and urged individuals, schools and communities to reduce negative outcomes by altering risks or exposure to risks that could be addressed such as childhood poverty, hunger, lack of early education, or dangerous aspects of a community setting. These steps helped to reduce the negative chain reaction following risk exposure, including breaking cycles of poverty, teen pregnancy, and substance abuse (Rutter, 1987). Programs that helped youth establish and maintain self-esteem and self-efficacy and opened up opportunities for increased personal responsibility were also deemed protective in nature (Rutter, 1987).

One program in particular found success by rooting their efforts in social-emotional education and community support (City of Minneapolis, 2012). At the individual level, children were offered opportunities to develop attachment relationships through caring teachers and mentors, and they were taught "positive self-talk" to increase a sense of mastery of skills and attitudes (City of Minneapolis, 2012). There was direct emphasis on building social competencies as well as academic skills. At the community level, "avoiding the avoidable" was practiced, through reducing stressors that do not need to be faced and generating resources to support children's needs (City of Minneapolis, 2012).

Addressing Mental Health Issues

The current state of affairs in schools' responses to students' mental health issues includes staff who have received too little training to adequately and swiftly recognize serious problems; too little time during the teaching schedule to pay close attention to emotional and psychological issues; and too few resources, including money, to address even those issues that are identified (Anderson, 2016).

Even when there is adequate staffing, there often is a lack of clarity as to whose job it is to deal with various aspects of the mental health puzzle. Teachers feel that they are not trained to be psychologists or counselors; yet, teachers are the best front-line defense against the escalation of mental health problems since they know their students the best and are in a daily position to observe their behaviors (Anderson, 2016).

How Schools Can Help

Most everyone agrees that the school mental health crisis cannot be addressed without a team approach, more technically known as a "multi-tiered system of supports" (Rosen, 2018; National Association of School Psychologists,

2016). This model of care can be visualized as the upside-down pyramid or funnel with a broad, general approach to student mental health and wellbeing, funneling to a more specialized, clinical care for those students who need it; everyone in the school community is part of the broad team response, while the specialists and clinicians address the more serious and technical problems (Rosen, 2018). Some schools have taken steps to create what are called "trauma informed schools" (Berger, 2018).

Trauma-Informed Schools

Trauma-informed schools are those whose educators, administrators, and other school personnel are aware of the impact of trauma on students and its myriad influences on their behavior, relationships, and ability to regulate internal states and how that plays out in the classroom (Walkley & Cox, 2013; McInernery & McKlindon, 2015). Trauma-informed schools understand that a student's behavior is a developmental response to his or her past experience; this understanding leads educators to ask questions about what might have happened to that child to cause the resulting behaviors, rather than centering on questions such as "what is wrong with this child?" (McInerney & McKlindon, 2015).

Such a stance, when practiced throughout a school, helps all staff begin to think in different ways about addressing the underlying needs that any particular child may have. In a seminar online, Kaufman (2013) made the following observation:

> When we think about components of a trauma-informed school, it's important, and I think very helpful, to look at a multi-tiered approach. So, what's happening universally on the school campus? What kinds of positive behavior interventions and supports are in place to support all students and support a healthy, safe, and compassionate school climate? What kinds of supports are in place in terms of teaching social-emotional learning, and how do we begin to recognize that in the trauma-informed school environment all children are supported regardless of trauma history? Often, we may not know who of the student body has been exposed, but certainly, if we're providing a safe and sane and secure and caring climate, it will ultimately support all students (n.p.).

The multitiered approach to student mental health is beginning with a universal level of care for all students that then narrows into the secondary or more selective tier at which small groups work to address some of the symptoms of child trauma in a more targeted population (Kaufman, 2013). This entails both mental health intervention as well as addressing behavioral issues through a thoughtful approach to disciplinary policies and procedures--ones that begin to take into account some of the child's past experience and see school responses in ways that transcend disciplinary or punitive standpoints (Walkley & Cox, 2013). An example of such an approach might be the use of the restorative justice protocol (Restorative Justice Council, 2011).

At the most intensive level of care, schools need to move to available partnerships with those individuals, organizations, and agencies that can provide necessary mental health services. It is essential to access providers who are able to provide the one-on-one mental health services necessary to help students who have experienced various forms trauma and are presenting significant symptomatology (McInernery & McKlindon, 2015).

Identification

A hallmark of a high functioning trauma-informed school is that it can identify students who need higher levels of intervention before behaviors become problematic (Berger, 2018). This involves screening, obviously, but screening often identifies more obvious, observable, external behaviors, while much of the damage from trauma can be expressed internally, in more subtle ways (McInernery & McKlindon, 2015). It is sometimes difficult for those doing the screening to be aware of deeper-lurking problems.

Staff must be trained to take note of not just externalized behaviors in a classroom or other school setting but must be cognizant of less-overt signs such as disengagement or withdrawal that can indicate student problems (Walkley & Cox, 2013). Most staff referrals are of the overt nature, but the effectiveness of a school program lies in being able to notice and make referrals for less obvious behavior as well (Berger, 2018).

In an ideal scenario, schools would be able to provide universal screening involving entire grade levels or entire classrooms (Benevento, 2018). This technique removes the stigma of singling out individual students for further scrutiny. Even when schools are able to implement universal screening, however, many do not have the available resources to meet the needs they find. Adopting more targeted approaches becomes necessary; scrutinizing factors such as test scores, grade patterns, attendance records, disciplinary referrals, or other variables can act as a starting point (Benevento, 2018). Anecdotal information and observational material augment the "harder" data to comprise a fuller picture of student functioning.

Training and Support

Most teachers, administrators and school staff beyond guidance and school psychologists have had little to no training in the principles of childhood trauma, identification, and intervention (Pickens & Tschopp, 2017). If schools are to view these professionals as first-line defense against conditions that can lead to school violence, there is a need for quality training for all. Such education is also essential in teacher and administrator preparation programs, as too often, this information is reserved for counselor training only.

As educators become more astute and involved in recognition of the pain and suffering of many of their students, they put themselves at further risk of vicarious trauma, or what has been termed "compassion fatigue" (American Institute of Stress, 2018). Understanding that school personnel can be impacted by the stories and life experiences that students carry with them is critical to school-wide well-being and effective intervention.

Raising staff awareness and implementing strategies that bolster and encourage professionals' self-care is a first step (Kaufman, 2013). This can be as simple as a discussion, healthy food and reading selections strategically placed in the staff lounge, and "certainly understanding the ways in which trauma-informed systems can also become trauma-exposed systems" (Kaufman, 2013, n.p.).

Kaufman (2013) also notes the necessity of thinking inclusively about what constitutes school staff, as students often have close relationships with bus drivers, the custodial staff and the cafeteria staff, as well as office technicians, the school nurse, librarians, and the other school aides and support personnel. With proper education, these individuals can be in unique places to recognize and respond to children in crisis, thus creating a school-wide safety net of informed and caring personnel (McInernery & McKlindon, 2015).

Resiliency and Mental Health

Another approach is that of building resiliency in students (Parker & Folkman, 2015). As early as the 1990s many counselors and educators were researching and touting the importance of nurturing traits of resiliency in students, both to buffer them against life's stressors and addressing childhood insults that their environments may have exposed them to. This also marked a major shift in studying "at risk" children—moving from psychogenesis to salutogenesis—a focus on health rather than pathology (Bauer, 2017). Resilience research, even in its infancy, was centered on the traits, coping skills, and supports that help children survive, or even thrive, in challenging environments (Parker & Folkman, 2015).

While there are many different definitions of resiliency, they share common elements. Werner and Smith (1992), who conducted seminal, longitudinal research on the topic, noted that the traits of positive mental health and prosocial behaviors were such that "the resilient child is one who works well, plays well, loves well, and expects well" (p. 192). Masten (2018) describes resiliency as the capacity of a system to adapt successfully to threats to its viability, function, or development. The goal of resiliency work is to build humans' capacity to adapt.

Rather than a trait or capacity, resilience is a process to harness resources to sustain well-being (Masten, 2018). The human capacity to harness resources leads to a consideration of what specific resources are needed in different situations and environments to promote well-being (Masten, 2018).

Werner and Smith (1992) discussed resilient schools as early as 1982. The characteristics of such schools begin with accepting each child's temperamental idiosyncrasies and allowing them to face some challenges, without overwhelming their coping abilities when faced with those challenges (Werner & Smith, 1992). This entails knowing each child well so that challenges stretch but do not crush him or her. A second element is to convey to children a sense of responsibility and caring for others and the learning environment; they should be rewarded for positive incidents of helpfulness and cooperation (Werner & Smith, 1992).

Werner & Smith (1982) defined a foundational practice of resilient schools as encouraging each student to develop special interests, hobbies, or activities that can serve as a source of self-gratification and self-esteem. Educators within resilient schools also model, by example and in their curriculum, a belief that life makes sense even in the face of the inevitable adversities that each member encounters (Werner & Smith, 1982). Resilient schools also encourage and provide opportunities for children to be able to tap the resources of individuals beyond their nuclear family—relatives, friends, teachers, mentors, or community members (Werner & Smith, 1992).

It is interesting to note that the American Academy of Pediatrics (2018) lists "the absence of the buffering protection of a supportive, adult relationship" (n.p.) as the single most important mediating factor in how a child will respond to an adverse childhood experience. Resilient schools can play a powerful role in combating toxic stress and trauma through cultivating such buffering relationships in a variety of ways, such as formal mentoring, coaching, job shadowing, apprenticeships, and the presence of caring teachers and staff (McInernery & McKlindon, 2015).

The Role of Action in Healing from Trauma

Recent school shootings have again reinforced the role of action in helping victims of trauma to heal. As far back as the Columbine High School shootings, survivors and family members of those killed and wounded decided to turn their grief into outward actions that both honored the victims and helped themselves turn their emotions into positive growth through helping others. As the result of the traumatic loss of Rachel Scott, the first student killed in the Columbine shooting massacre, her family created Rachel's Challenge as a way to encourage students to show more compassion toward each other (Rachel's Challenge, n.d.a).

More recently, students from Parkland and Santa Fe have turned to activism as a way of reacting to trauma (Mekouar, 2018). Earlier studies of resiliency illustrated that righteous anger can become a buoy, whereas passive acceptance of adverse circumstances can lead to internalized emotions and depression (Gordon & Song, 1994). Gordon & Song (1994) spoke of this as "healthy anger" and found that study participants who were "defiers of negative prediction" (p. 36) saw change as possible and rewarding, so that they were willing to act in situations that might appear overly challenging and overwhelming to others. Several parents of Parkland victims have decided to run for school board, channeling their frustration and grief into what they hope will be lasting change, while students have rallied and lobbied, planning events such as March for our Lives Day and a "die in" event in Washington, DC (Mekouar, 2018). In action, they have found an outlet for their emotions and an opportunity to make a positive impact (Jonsson, 2018).

Need for Prevention Rather than Reaction

According to Walker (2018), a recent Duke University study that included more than 10,000 American teenagers concluded that more than 50 percent of adolescents with psychiatric disorders go untreated and for those fortunate enough to receive some form of treatment, schools are the most likely source. This is encouraging on the one hand, but troubling on the other, as school budgets are so often cut and vital services become scarce. Unfortunately, psychiatric conditions are not taken seriously, and they are inextricably "linked to a whole host of other problems" (Costello, as cited in Walker, 2018, p. 1).

Despite the fact that U.S. schools have been forced to become the de facto mental health system for so many of this nation's school-aged children, there is a dearth of trained and licensed counselors who have the luxury of being a regular presence at their schools (Anderson & Cardoza, 2016). Mental health professionals too frequently are rotated among schools, if available at all, and their student numbers have increased, making it difficult to know students well and attend to an overwhelming caseload (Anderson & Cardoza, 2016; Anderson, 2016). While early and proper diagnosis of mental health conditions may be the key to promoting school safety, the NEA notes dramatic cuts in funding for school counselors, school social workers, and school psychologists (Walker, 2018).

After Sandy Hook and the loss of its young victims, national interest in improving student mental health services was reignited and became a seminal element in the Obama administration's comprehensive plan to address school violence (Strauss, 2013). The proposal included $150 million for school-based resource officers and mental health professionals, $50 million for training new social workers, and $15 million in new funding to train teachers in "mental-health first aid" (Walker, 2018). These initiatives became mired in a legislative war over gun control (Strauss, 2013).

In Walker's (2018) article, an expert on school crisis prevention and intervention at the University at Buffalo revealed that school districts have an obligation to take a more expansive view of what improves school safety. While so many schools have responded to shootings and other acts of school violence with greater police presence, more school resource officers, and more sophisticated surveillance technology, Nickerson (as cited in Walker, 2018) remarks:

> I'm always astounded as we are cutting mental health staff and social workers and school psychologists and others, and then we're going to spend money on hard-wired security," Nickerson told The Buffalo News. "I'm not saying that those things aren't important, but at the end of the day, if we look at the thwarted school shootings, that's almost always that somebody identified that there was a threat that was made, and they got the help that was needed (p. 1).

A 2013 State Legislation Report issued by the National Alliance on Mental Illness (NAMI) found that an improved economy allowed state legislatures to at least begin rebuilding mental health budgets that were decimated by the recession. Several states passed laws aimed at ensuring adequate access to care, and improving early intervention, school-based services and staff training; yet these gains are being threatened again by current budget proposals (NAMI, 2013).

The most effective programs create partnerships between schools and community organizations that can facilitate connections and provide a continuum of preventative care services (Anderson, 2016). Resources and expertise are pooled, making it easier to recognize when someone is troubled and requires help. Schools play a crucial part in this because their personnel have frequent contact with students and access to observation of student behavior on a regular basis (Anderson, 2016).

They also provide a less threatening environment for the student; this is particularly true in schools that foster strong relationships between and among school members where a level of trust has developed between staff, students and families that may not necessarily exist with other providers (Anderson, 2016). While these facts illustrate the critical role that schools can play, they cannot combat the mental health crisis alone.

FINAL THOUGHTS

It is clear that schools are grappling with more mental health issues among their student population than ever before. These issues have implications for both academic achievement and school culture, including developing and maintaining a culture of student safety and perceived well-being. With most experts agreeing that at least 20 percent of a given school's population will have diagnosed mental health disorders (and higher percentages among urban and schools set in impoverished neighborhoods), it is no wonder that schools struggle to meet both their academic vision and the everyday mental health realities of their populations (Crary, 2014). Most school districts have seen an increased need for mental health services and decreased resources simultaneously, rendering them even less capable of addressing the epidemic.

Historically, our nation's schools have served as the de facto dispenser of mental health services for the vast majority of students, especially those who are low-income. This urgent need makes it essential that schools form partnerships with parents and community agencies to make certain that students with disorders do not fall through the cracks. Teachers and preservice teacher trainers need to become comfortable with a more intentional curriculum to discuss, identify, and address student needs. The stigma around mental illness can be diminished once schools take a more proactive, educational stance toward prevalent conditions that threaten students' well-being, connectedness, and achievement.

Fortunately, as future chapters will propose, there is much that we know about how to bolster students' health and well-being that can promote prosocial interactions and decrease the risk of security threats to our schools. This includes incorporating health and wellness curriculum and activities into the school day, talking in informational and compassionate ways about mental illness and its effects, building resiliency and student assets, developing meaningful relationships with all students so that they feel connected to the school community, presenting an engaging curriculum that meets the needs of diverse learners, and bridging gaps in services through powerful partnerships with community and other agencies.

POINTS TO REMEMBER

- *It is estimated that 20 percent of current school-aged children and adolescents suffer from some kind of mental health issue.*
- *Mental health problems affect school performance, both academically and socially, and are evidenced in such symptoms as poor attendance, inability to concentrate or attend to learning, poor relationships with teachers and*

peers, anxiety that affects academic performance, or withdrawal from the daily life of the school.
- *The most frequently evidenced mental health disorders among schoolchildren are PTSD, anxiety, depression, mood disorders, ADHD, conduct disorder, oppositional defiant disorder, a wide array of autism spectrum disorders, eating disorders, and Tourette Syndrome.*
- *Those afflicted with mental illness, especially if combined with substance abuse, are at higher risk to pose school safety threats through violent acts toward others and self.*
- *Mental health disorders can emanate from biological, environmental or a combination of both factors.*
- *Mental health is affected by both risk and protective factors; in order to promote good mental health, we need to reduce children's risk factors and boost the protective ones.*
- *Research has shown that student connectedness and engagement within the school setting is critical in prosocial behavior, leading to decreased school disruption or violence.*
- *There are strategies (to be discussed in upcoming chapters) for building student engagement, relational connectedness, resiliency and mental and emotional well-being that can be incorporated into any school.*

Chapter 4

Protocols and Preemptive Preparation

Effective Interventions that Support Students

School violence, particularly high-profile school shootings, may cause concern within all school communities, even those that are not directly affected by the violent event. Administrators, teachers, students, parents, and community members continually struggle to understand why such violent events happen and how they can be prevented. School principals and superintendents can reassure students, staff, and parents that schools are indeed safe places for children and reiterate what safety measures and student supports are already in place in their school (National Association of School Psychologists [NASP], School Safety and Crisis Response Committee, 2015; NASP, 2017).

STRATEGIES FOR CREATING SCHOOL SAFETY

To maintain safety and a positive, successful learning environment, schools require consistent and effective approaches that prevent violence and promote learning, adequate time to implement these approaches, and ongoing evaluation (Cowan, Vaillancourt, Rossen, & Pollitt, 2013). Safe and successful learning environments are cultivated by collaboration among school staff and community-based service providers and by the impartation of equivalent resources to support instructional components, organizational/management components, and learning supports (Cowan et al., 2013).

To create safe schools, purposeful and coordinated strategies must be implemented to increase levels of safety and security that simultaneously promote student wellness and resilience, improve students' readiness to learn, and build positive school climates (NASP, 2017). Efforts to reduce school violence that use multiple strategies selected specifically for each school's needs that require collaboration among administrators, teachers, school psychologists, school resource officers, parents, students, and the local community are the most successful (NASP, 2017).

Needs Assessment

Schools should endeavor to conduct a needs assessment in order to select and plan for the implementation of school violence safety programs and interventions that are geared toward the school's specific needs (NASP, 2017). A needs assessment will assist administrators in identifying a school's strengths and risks; for example, it might reveal what types of violence can occur, the context in which it occurs, frequent classes of victims, and the effectiveness of any existing disciplinary measures and intervention efforts (NASP, 2017). In addition, the needs assessment should examine administrators' and educators' specific strengths and existing resources to help guide decisions in not only program and strategy selection, but professional development opportunities (NASP, 2017).

Crisis Response Plans

It is critical to establish comprehensive school crisis response plans for a multitude of emergency situations that include clearly defined roles for each member of the multidisciplinary crisis team (NASP, 2017; National School Safety and Security Services, 2018). Plans should have explicit procedures for reaffirming physical health, safeguarding perceptions of safety, regenerating social support, assessing psychological trauma risk, and delivering appropriate interventions based on the level of risk (NASP, 2017).

Balance Physical and Psychological Safety

Although armed violence by intruders is extremely rare, it can be extremely difficult to prevent and solutions such as metal detectors and armed security officers are not always the most effective methods of prevention (NASP, 2017). Barricading schools against all possible means of harm is actually counterproductive to maintaining a healthy learning environment and may even undermine it (NASP, 2017; Cowan et al., 2013). Reasonable physical security, such as locked doors, lighted and monitored hallways, and visitor reporting systems, combined with violence prevention and positive behavior supports, are much more likely to promote and maintain a healthy learning environment (NASP, 2017).

School Climate

Positive school climates that promote learning, psychological health, and student success should be created and maintained by balancing physical security with efforts that cultivate student resiliency, connectedness, and social competency (Benbenishty, Astor, Roziner, & Wrabel, 2016). Helping students feel valued and personally invested in keeping their schools safe is vital to this effort. Fostering and promoting trusting student-adult relationships is essential to empowering students to take responsibility to report potentially dangerous activity (NASP, 2017).

School Discipline

Effective, positive school discipline allows students to feel respected and supported, reinforces positive behavior, and improves school climate (Benbenishty et al., 2016). Overly harsh and punitive measures, such as zero-tolerance policies, lead to reduced safety, feelings of connectedness, and have historically been unsuccessful at improving student behavior or school climate (Cowan et al., 2013).

There is also an ongoing debate whether the use of school resource officers is inappropriate, contributes to safety and the perception of feeling safe, and perpetuates the school-to-prison pipeline (Cowan et al., 2013). School discipline should be used as a learning opportunity to teach and reinforce positive behaviors and safeguard the well-being of all students, while discipline measures should be clear, consistent, equitably applied to all students, and employ culturally competent practices (Cowan et al., 2013).

Prevention Programs

School-wide anti-violence initiatives and violence prevention programs that encourage positive emotional student development and the use of nonviolent conflict resolution strategies should be implemented by and promoted within schools. These programs serve as a natural bridge between individual change interventions and those that establish positive school climates and cultures (NASP, 2017; Centers for Disease Control and Prevention, 2017).

Mental Health Services

Mental health, behavior, safety, and learning are all an integral part of a student's school experience; therefore, schools should provide adequate access to mental health services (NASP, 2017). With many schools having inadequate mental health coverage, administrators should advocate for more school psychologists, counselors, and social workers that can offer assessment and counseling to students and can consult with families and teachers to provide effective interventions and supports (NASP, 2017).

Cross Collaboration

There are many students that experience significant school behavioral adjustment problems and strategies should be implemented that foster the social-emotional skills associated with adaptive coping and resilience (NASP, 2017; CASEL, 2018). Students face complex issues and, as a result, experience social and/or psychological distress that may require the coordination of interventions across school and community agencies, such as juvenile probation, child welfare services, and alcohol and drug treatment (NASP, 2017).

Systematic Response to Threats

Every threat must be reviewed, and threat response efforts made by the school should be based on research-validated procedures and include collaboration and communication with educators, mental health professionals, and law enforcement agencies (NASP, 2017). Schools must respond to all threats that are made using a threat assessment approach to evaluate and intervene against any potential violent behavior (Stewart & Mohandie, 2014). While research does show that the vast majority of student threats do not result in violence, the threats do provide an opportunity for schools to understand and respond to the needs of those students making the threats and those that are the recipients of them (Stewart & Mohandie, 2014; NASP, 2017).

KEY LEADERSHIP ROLES IN SCHOOL SAFETY

School Principals

School leaders must mobilize school staff, students, parents, and the local community around the school's mission, shared values, and school improvement goals. School principals should aspire to build consensus on a vision that reflects school safety as a core value of the school community and support student safety and well-being (Cowan et al., 2013). Principals are in the unique position to develop a learning culture that is adaptive, collaborative, innovative, and supportive by taking into consideration the contributions of every member of the school staff (Cowan & Paine, 2013).

School-Employed Mental Health Professionals

There are many school-employed mental health professionals that serve in critical leadership roles in terms of school safety, positive school climate, and providing school-based mental health services, whose training and expertise help link mental health, behavior, environmental factors, instruction, and learning (Cowan et al., 2013). Each of these professionals helps create school environments that are safe, supportive, and conducive to learning and although they may provide similar services, they each have their own unique focus that results in different, interrelated services (Cowan & Paine, 2013).

School Counselors

School counselors are often the first school-employed mental health professionals to interact with students as they have specialized knowledge of curriculum and instruction and are able to help students with their academic, personal/social, and career development goals (Cowan et al., 2013).

Counseling programs are designed to be a collaborative effort between the school counselor, teachers, families, and students to create an environment that promotes student success, active engagement, and equitable access to educational opportunities (Cowan & Paine, 2013). In their role, school counselors also work to promote safe learning environments for the larger school community and regularly monitor and respond to any behavior issues that may impact the school climate (Cowan et al., 2013; Cowan & Paine, 2013).

School Psychologists

School psychologists have extensive knowledge of learning, motivation, behavior, disabilities, assessment, evaluation, and school law, and specialize in analyzing complex problems and selecting and implementing appropriate evidence-based interventions (Cowan & Paine, 2013). They also regularly consult with teachers and parents to provide coordinated services and supports for students struggling with learning disabilities, emotional and behavioral problems, anxiety/depression, and emotional trauma (Cowan et al., 2013).

As regular members of school crisis teams, school psychologists collaborate with school administrators and other educators to prevent and respond to crises and conduct risk and threat assessments to identify students at risk of harming themselves or others (Cowan et al., 2013; Cowan & Paine, 2013).

School Social Workers

School social workers have special expertise in understanding family and community systems and linking students and their families with community services essential for promoting student success (Cowan & Paine, 2013). Using their knowledge of, and training in, cultural diversity, systems theory, social justice, risk assessment and intervention, consultation and collaboration, and clinical intervention strategies, school social workers are able to address the mental health and social needs of students and ease any barriers to learning that were created as a result of poverty, inadequate health care, and neighborhood violence (Cowan et al., 2013).

In their role, school social workers act in conjunction with teachers, administrators, and parents to provide coordinated interventions to vulnerable student populations that are designed to help their families access the supports needed to promote student success (Cowan & Paine, 2013).

School Resource Officers

School resource officers have a duty to protect students and staff on school grounds and bring specialized knowledge of the law, local and national crime trends and safety threats, and the local juvenile justice system (Cowan et al., 2013). Officers also serve as critical members of schools' policy-making teams on environmental safety planning and facilities management, school-safety policy, and emergency response preparedness (Cowan et al., 2013).

THREAT ASSESSMENT

Threat assessment is an important element of an all-inclusive approach to school safety and violence prevention that offers schools an alternative to ineffective and counterproductive zero-tolerance discipline policies and procedures (NASP, 2014). Threat assessment involves the ability to identify student threats to commit a violent act, determine the seriousness of the threat, and develop intervention strategies that protect potential victims and address the underlying problem that motivated the threatening behavior (NASP, 2014).

Effective threat assessment teams seek not only to keep schools safe but to assist potential offenders in surmounting the underlying causes of their anger, hopelessness, or despair (NASP, 2014; National School Safety and Security Services, 2018). As members of threat assessment teams, school psychologists evaluate a student's need for educational and psychological services, gather information on the student's motives and reasons behind the threat, provide school officials with the necessary information about the student's resources and risks for violence, and make recommendations that meet the student's needs and resolve the problem that caused the threatening behavior (NASP, 2014).

Threat Assessment Approaches and Implementation in Schools

Threats of violence must be taken seriously by school administrators and educators and effective procedures to assess any threats should include established district-wide policies and procedures that clarify the role educators take in relation to law enforcement and specifically identify the threat assessment team and their training (NASP, 2014). Interdisciplinary threat assessment teams should include a compilation of effort between administrators, school-employed mental health professionals, and law enforcement in order to improve efficiency and reduce the risk of bias (National School Safety and Security Services, 2018).

The implementation of a threat assessment approach centers on educating the larger school community on the importance of a positive school climate that aids students before problems escalate into violence (NASP, 2014). Written materials should be made available to the public explaining the relevant aspects of the threat assessment policy to staff members, students, and families (NASP, 2017). Regular assessments of school climate should also be conducted with emphasis on students' levels of trust in school staff and their willingness to request help with any problems that may be occurring (NASP, 2017).

Referrals to appropriate mental health and social services, as well as a follow-up system on the effectiveness of the intervention, should be included in schools' threat assessment processes (NASP, 2017). Threat assessment approaches can provide a valuable opportunity for educators to identify students that are at risk for mental health problems and provide them with the necessary and appropriate interventions and supports (NASP, 2017).

Research has shown a number of additional positive outcomes as a result of using a threat assessment approach including a reduction in bullying, increased perceptions of a positive and supportive school climate, greater willingness to seek help, and fewer long-term suspensions (NASP, 2017; NASP, 2014). Threat assessment approaches have also demonstrated a valuable opportunity to identify students at risk for a variety of mental health problems and guide appropriate interventions and supports.

MULTI-TIERED SYSTEMS OF SUPPORTS (MTSS)

Rather than viewing school safety as a targeted outcome of a single or standalone program/plan, the Multi-tiered Systems of Support Model strives to integrate all services for students and families by enclosing the necessary behavioral, mental health, and social services within the context of a school's culture and learning environment (Rosen, 2018). Research has shown that an integration of services can lead to a more sustainable and comprehensive school improvement, a reduction of duplicative efforts, and a greater commitment to leadership (Cowan et al., 2013).

MTSS encompass prevention, wellness promotion, and interventions that increase with intensity based on student need and promote close school-community collaboration (Rosen, 2018). Under MTSS, a universal screening procedure is used to determine academic, behavioral, and emotional barriers to learning, monitor ongoing student progress in response to implemented interventions, and enable administrators to use systematic data-based decision making to determine what services are needed for students based on specific outcomes (Cowan et al., 2013; Benevento, 2018).

Ideally, MTSS is wholistically implemented to integrate efforts targeting academic, behavioral, social, emotional, physical, and mental health concerns yet schools across the country are using response to intervention (RTI) and positive behavior interventions and supports (PBIS) as their primary methods for implementing an MTSS framework (Rosen, 2018). Research has found that the MTSS framework is more effective in coordinating school-employed and community-based service providers and ensuring the integration and coordination of services among a student's school, home, and community (Cowan et al., 2013).

In order for the MTSS framework to be effective, adequate access to school-employed specialized instructional support personnel, such as school counselors, psychologists, social workers, and nurses, and community-based services is required (Cowan et al., 2013). Adequate time for planning, collaborating, and problem solving is also needed to integrate effective services and time for the collection, evaluation, interpretation, and use of data is a must (Cowan et al., 2013).

Research supports the fact that access to school-based mental health services directly improves students' physical and psychological safety, academic performance, and social-emotional learning and as such, an adequate number of mental health professionals should be employed by schools (Cowan et al., 2013). Access to school mental health services must be consistent and connected to the learning process and school-employed mental health professionals are expressly trained in the interconnectivity among school law, school system functioning, learning, mental health, and family systems (Cowan, Vaillancourt, Rossen, & Pollitt, 2013).

It is this unique training that ensures students receive proper and effective services that are infused into the learning environment and supports teachers' abilities to provide a safe school setting and optimum conditions for teaching and learning (Rosen, 2018; Cowan et al., 2013). Mental health professionals also work collaboratively to provide a wider range of services to students that can include the design and implementation of interventions to meet student behavioral and mental health needs, individual and group counseling sessions, staff development related to positive discipline, behavior, and mental health, and risk and threat assessments (Cowan et al., 2013).

STRATEGIES TO REINFORCE SCHOOL SAFETY

Administrators should stress the significance of a caring school community where educators and students respect and trust each other, and all students feel connected, understand expectations, and receive the behavioral and mental health support they need (NASP School Safety and Crisis Response Committee, 2015; NASP, 2017). Sending messages to the local community and parents following a violent event will reassure everyone about the safety of their school.

There are a variety of ways in which administrators can reinforce that schools are safe environments and increase student/adult comfort levels following a violent incident or crisis.

- Principals may write a letter to parents explaining school safety policies and crisis prevention efforts and cite appropriate statistics related to school safety and overall rates of violence within schools.
- A press release might also be issued regarding the school district's efforts to maintain safe and caring schools through clear behavioral expectations, positive behavior interventions and supports, and crisis planning and preparedness.
- Violence prevention programs and the current curriculum should be emphasized as well as the efforts the school is making to teach students alternatives to violence.
- A formal review of all school-safety policies and procedures should be conducted to ensure that developing school safety issues are sufficiently addressed in current school crisis plans and emergency response procedures.
- Communication systems should also be reviewed with community responders, particularly for how the school will inform parents in the event of an emergency. (NASP School Safety and Crisis Response Committee, 2015; NASP, 2017)

Physical Safety

Schools should ensure that there is limited access to school buildings and designate one entrance as the main entrance while locking all other access points from the inside. Upon entrance to the building, guests must report to the main office, sign in, and wear a badge identifying that they are familiar to the school and belong there (NASP School Safety and Crisis Response

Committee, 2015; AiRISTA Flow, 2016; National School Safety and Security Services, 2018).

Security monitors should be installed to patrol the school parking lot and particular note should be made of those that enter and leave school grounds. In addition, hallways, cafeterias, and playgrounds should be monitored by school staff members at all times with school resource officers patrolling the greater campus area (NASP School Safety and Crisis Response Committee, 2015; AiRISTA Flow, 2016).

Proactive School Systems

Schools should endeavor to promote compliance with school rules and set forth school-wide behavioral expectations at the start of each school year (Positive Behaviors, Interventions & Supports, 2018). Positive interventions and supports, psychological and counseling services, and violence prevention programs that include bully-proofing, social skill development, and conflict mediation should also be in place and address the necessity of students acting responsibly and encourage them to report potential problems before they occur (Positive Behaviors, Interventions & Supports, 2018; NASP School Safety and Crisis Response Committee, 2015).

Participation by Students

Students must be encouraged to take responsibility for their part in keeping schools safe, including active participation in safety planning as they know better than school staff the areas in school that are more likely to be dangerous and a breeding ground for school violence to occur (NASP School Safety and Crisis Response Committee, 2015; NASP, 2017; Cowan et al., 2013).

Key Points in Talking with Students

Students' questions should guide what and how much information a school provides. Administrators and teachers should talk openly with students to validate their feelings and be honest about their own feelings related to violence (NASP School Safety and Crisis Response Committee, 2015). Students will not always talk about their feelings readily and teachers should be patient and monitor students closely for clues that they may want to talk, particularly for those students who would rather express their feelings in writing, music, or art projects instead (NASP School Safety and Crisis Response Committee, 2015).

Most importantly, administrators and teachers should be aware of student distress signals, such as changes in behavior, anxiety/depression, energy level, acting out, and/or problems at school or with academics (NASP School

Safety and Crisis Response Committee, 2015). Teachers and parents should also be conscious of media exposure and what they personally say about any events that may have occurred at school, or any other school, and television viewing should be limited if allowed to be on in school common areas (NASP School Safety and Crisis Response Committee, 2015).

Students should be reminded that schools are generally safe places and that their teachers actively engage with local police and fire departments, emergency responders, and hospitals to keep them safe (NASP School safety and Crisis Response Committee, 2015). It is important to share that while there is no absolute guarantee that a school will remain totally safe, there is a difference between the possibility of a violent act occurring and the probability that it will actually affect them and their school (Kamerman & Blumenthal, 2018). Students should also be reminded that they play an essential role in school safety and that they should be vigilant in their observations and report anything they see or hear that makes them uncomfortable, nervous, or frightened (Kamerman & Blumenthal, 2018).

The difference between reporting, tattling or gossiping should be made clear to students and that they can provide important information, either directly or anonymously, that may prevent harm (NASP School Safety and Crisis Response Committee, 2015). When students participate in antiviolence programs, learn conflict mediation skills, and seek help from others when they, or someone else, is struggling with anger, depression, or other uncontrollable emotions, they can be an active part of a positive solution (Kamerman & Blumenthal, 2018).

If an act of violence were to occur, it would be almost impossible to understand why it happened and what provoked someone to do such a terrible thing. Students should understand that sometimes people do things to hurt other people, perhaps due to their inability to handle anger, as a result of being under the influence of drugs or alcohol, or they are suffering from a mental illness (NASP School Safety and Crisis Response Committee, 2015).

It is important that students know how to get help if they are angry or upset and to stay away from drugs, alcohol, guns, and other weapons. Doing things that they enjoy, staying with their normal routine, and being with friends and family can help make students feel more at ease about an event that has occurred or worry less that an event will occur (NASP School Safety and Crisis Response Committee, 2015).

CRISIS PREVENTION AND INTERVENTION TRAINING

Schools play a critical role in crisis prevention and are responsible for meeting the needs of students, staff, families, and the local community (NASP,

2017; Lazzaro, Brock, & Dwyer, 2014). Crises in schools can range from natural disasters and acts of terrorism to school and community violence, death, and even suicide, and it is expected that schools are prepared to meet the needs of students, staff, and families as well as collaborate with local community agencies during these time (Lazzaro et al., 2014; U.S. Department of Education, 2016).

In response, the majority of schools have implemented safety and security procedures and developed programs to promote mental health, prevention and intervention policies, and appropriate community resources in their safety plans (Lazzaro et al., 2014). Developing comprehensive crisis plans that best fit the unique needs of each school is strongly dependent upon training and resources and thus, training and preparedness are critical to effective response efforts (Lazzaro et al., 2014; U.S. Department of Education, 2016).

School staff members should participate in annual training and simulation drills, including intruder alerts and weather and fire emergencies, and building level teams should regularly review crisis and emergency plans so that teachers and other staff will know how to respond to students' questions and support them during, and after, a crisis event (U.S. Department of Education, 2016; National School Safety and Security Services, 2018).

As seen with the most recent crisis events, schools are integral to an overall community crisis response by providing a safe haven of normalcy, disseminating information, identifying at-risk individuals, providing mental health services, and referring to community service agencies when necessary (NASP, 2017). To serve in this capacity, schools must have short and long-term crisis plans and teams in place that encompass preparedness, prevention, response and recovery (U.S. Department of Education, 2016).

Teams must be adequately trained in the various types of crises, systems, and procedures, as well as the unique mental health needs that can occur in times of crisis (NASP, 2017). Plans must also be clearly communicated to educators and parents and fully incorporate the efforts of community emergency response agencies and health and mental service providers (NASP, 2017; Lazzaro et al., 2014).

Schools inherently have unique opportunities and challenges in preventing and responding to violence and crises. As such, training for school crisis teams must address acts of violence as a mental health, physical health, and safety risk within the context of the individual school's culture (NASP, 2017).

Professional development programs, such as the PREPaRE School Crisis Prevention and Intervention Training Curriculum have been created to provide school-based mental health professionals, and other educational professionals, the necessary training on the roles and responsibilities that come with being a member of a school safety and crisis team (National Association of School Psychologists [NASP], 2013a).

PREPaRE

PREPaRE is one of the first comprehensive national training curriculums developed by school-based professionals and is based on the assumptions that (1) educators' skills are best utilized within a multidisciplinary team that engages in crisis prevention, preparedness, response, and recovery; (2) school crisis management is unique and requires its own conceptual model; and (3) school-based mental health professionals are best prepared to address any psychological issues that arise from school crises (NASP, 2013a).

More specifically, the PREPaRE (NASP, 2013a) model emphasizes that mental health professionals who are part of a school safety and crisis team should abide by a specific set of specific hierarchical and sequential set of activities to include

P—Prevent and PREPaRE for psychological trauma;
R—Reaffirm physical health and perceptions of security and safety;
E—Evaluate psychological trauma risk;
P—Provide interventions; a and;
R—Respond to psychological needs;
E—Examine the effectiveness of crisis prevention and intervention

The PREPaRE training curriculum enables schools to make prevention and intervention plans actionable and effective by having knowledgeable crisis intervention teams rooted in their schools (NASP, 2013a). The training curriculum addresses safety and the emotional and mental health aspects of crises and equips intervention teams with the necessary skills to conduct psychological triage and deliver a multi-tiered approach to the entire school community (Lazzaro et al., 2014).

FINAL THOUGHTS

Safe, positive, and successful school learning environments require individualized, effective, and collaborative approaches that prevent violence and promote learning. School climates that promote learning, psychological health, and student success can be created and maintained by balancing students' physical security with collaborative efforts that cultivate student resiliency, connectedness, and social competence. Empowering students to feel valued and personally invested in making their schools safe, as well as establishing student-teacher relationships of trust, is vital to any school's violence prevention efforts.

Mental health, behavior, safety, and learning are all interrelated and an integral part of a student's experience at school; therefore, particular focus should be placed on the ability of schools to provide adequate access to mental health services. School-employed mental health professionals are critical to school safety and the mental health services they can provide should be integrated with other behavioral and social services into a multi-tiered system of support that will directly improve students' physical and psychological safety, academic performance, and social-emotional learning.

POINTS TO REMEMBER

- *The most successful school violence prevention efforts are those that use strategies specific to the individual school's needs and require collaboration among administrators, teachers, school psychologists, school resource officers, parents, students, and the local community.*
- *Reasonable physical security efforts combined with violence prevention and positive behavior supports are more likely to promote and maintain a healthy learning environment.*
- *Students will feel respected and supported and exhibit more positive behavior in an improved school climate when positive school discipline is utilized by school officials. Threat assessment procedures give schools an alternative, all-inclusive approach to ineffective, punitive school disciplinary measures.*
- *Students can actively participate in school safety by reporting any action or statement that makes them uncomfortable, nervous, or frightened, learn conflict mediation skill, and know when to seek help for their own, or others', uncontrollable emotions.*

Chapter 5

Proactive and Protective Programs
Active Engagement to Foster School Safety

Students are able to confidently express their thoughts and ideas when schools are perceived as safe, positive learning environments and students and educators interact with respect and kindness (Towvim, Anderson, Thomas, & Blaisdell, 2012). Responding to student misbehavior and school violence with punishment alone can be isolating for students, resulting in feelings of alienation from peers and teachers, disengagement from school, and even dropping out of school altogether (Towvim et al., 2012). Complicating matters even further, research shows that sanctions, such as suspensions and expulsions, disproportionately affect African American students and students with emotional, behavioral, and learning disabilities (Loschert, 2016).

Research demonstrates that teaching positive behaviors to all students and modeling and reinforcing these behaviors leads to significant, favorable outcomes (Towvim et al., 2012). Evidence-based, school-wide programs that create an encouraging, supportive school climate, while mitigating and addressing negative behaviors have far-reaching and long-lasting benefits on school violence (Towvim et al., 2012).

To prevent school violence, it is imperative to understand the root causes, risks, and protective factors that are connected to it. Research has consistently explained bullying and violence in schools from an interpersonal and intrapersonal dynamic that largely depends on the understanding of how and why individuals engage in particular behaviors or respond in certain ways (Capp et al., 2017).

PUBLIC HEALTH STRATEGIES

Research shows that school violence can be prevented, and school environments can be improved through the efforts of teachers, administrators, parents, community members, and students (Centers for Disease Control and Prevention, 2017). No one factor can stop school violence completely; thus, prevention efforts should focus on reducing risk factors and promote protective factors at the individual, relationship, community, and societal level (Centers for Disease Control and Prevention, 2017). Among other interventions, public health strategies that focus on preventing violence before it starts have been shown to effectively reduce school violence (Centers for Disease Control and Violence Prevention, 2017).

Individual Strategies

Student skill level, knowledge, and experience influence whether they will become actively involved in violence and to significantly reduce this risk, their opportunities to participate in prosocial activities should be widened and their ability to effectively solve difficulties strengthened (Paolini, 2015). To address individual risks, school-based violence prevention programs should be embedded in a school's culture and focus on areas of "emotional self-awareness, emotional control, self-esteem, positive social skills, social problem-solving, conflict resolution, and teamwork" (Centers for Disease Control and Prevention, 2017, n.p.).

Relationship Strategies

Promoting positive relationships between families, teachers, and students are crucial to their well-being and preventing school violence. Ensuring that violence prevention programs are utilized school-wide and with fidelity increases the students' abilities to problem-solve independently and in groups, as well as promotes relationships between all inhabitants of the school and those who support them (Centers for Disease Control and Prevention, 2017).

Well-planned school-based programs and policies assist teachers in building "healthy relationships, model nonviolent attitudes and behaviors, and contribute to a broader positive school climate, which in turn lowers the risk for school violence" (Centers for Disease Control and Prevention, 2017, n.p.). Various approaches offer teachers classroom management and conflict-resolution strategies that promote positive relationships between all stakeholders. Involving families in both social and academic spheres ensures an overall school experience that is rich in communication and family unity, and has "substantial, long-term effects in reducing violent behavior" (Centers for Disease Control and Prevention, 2017, n.p.).

Community Level Strategies

A positive social environment at school can lessen the propensity for violence and schools can take a multitude of steps to ensure school connectedness and rigorous learning, while reducing negativity and possible violent outcomes. Some strategies to support a positive environment include diversity training, two-way communication, shared decision-making, the use of cooperative learning, and positive classroom management strategies (Centers for Disease Control and Prevention, 2017, n.p.).

The physical environment of a school can influence students' perceptions of fear and safety; thus,

> increasing natural surveillance, such as having windows at entrances . . . that does not block visibility . . . well-marked entrances and exits that are continually monitored . . . maintaining the building and parking areas by removing graffiti and making sure areas are well lit (Centers for Disease Control and Prevention, 2017, n.p.).

To increase monitoring and healthy skill development among students and reduce school violence, communities can help by providing students with "more structured and supervised after-school opportunities, such as mentoring programs or recreational activities" (Centers for Disease Control and Prevention, 2017, n.p.).

SOCIO-ECOLOGICAL APPROACH

Socio-ecological models of school violence integrate both external factors, such as poverty and crime, and internal characteristics and dynamics of schools, such as strong leadership and the readiness for change (Capp et al., 2017). There are many ecological layers that exert influence over school systems, whether they are cultural, religious, or political in nature (Capp et al., 2017). Individual behaviors of students, parents, teachers, and the local community all contribute to the overall safety of the school (Capp et al., 2017). Violence that occurs within schools, for example, may impact the surrounding community just as much as the violence in the surrounding community can affect the schools within it.

To appropriately and effectively address school violence and victimization, each layer of a very complex picture must be understood. Viewing and understanding a school from a socio-ecological standpoint allows administrators and educators to contemplate what school characteristics and dynamics are shared within certain contexts and what might be unique to a particular school setting (Capp et al., 2017).

By viewing school violence and safety through an ecological lens, schools are able to plan interventions that include multiple constituents and address what environmental and/or structural changes are needed to make schools safer (Capp et al., 2017). Learning what times and places within a particular school are susceptible to violence allows administrators to develop interventions that focus directly on those specific challenges (Capp et al., 2017).

EMPIRICALLY BASED PREVENTION AND INTERVENTION PROGRAMS

In an attempt to prevent school violence, every school should consider their own unique sociocultural influences, school climate, problems and severity of those problems (Capp et al., 2017). Without taking these factors and schools' individual needs into consideration, implementing the same intervention to prevent school violence at different schools is unlikely to adequately and effectively address issues of violence (Capp et al., 2017).

Promoting Alternative Thinking Strategies (PATHS) Program

The Promoting Alternative Thinking Strategies program is one of the highest-rated social-emotional learning and violence prevention programs by both the National Institute on Drug Abuse and the Office of Juvenile Justice and Delinquency Prevention for its strong evidence base, theoretical foundation, ease of implementation and reduction in aggression and behavior problems in students (Capp et al., 2017; Blueprints for Healthy Youth Development, 2018).

The PATHS program sets out to reduce aggression and problem behavior while promoting social and emotional competence and enhancing the educational process in grades K-6 (National Gang Center, 2018). There are five conceptual domains integrated into the PATHS lessons for each grade level that include self-control, emotional understanding, positive self-esteem, relationships, and interpersonal problem-solving skills (Blueprints for Healthy Youth Development, 2018).

As part of this program, teachers and school counselors undergo training and receive systematic and developmentally based lessons, materials and instructions for each grade level to teach students the five domains (Capp et al., 2017). PATHS is designed to be taught two-three times per week with daily activities that critically focus on facilitating the relationship between cognitive-affective understanding and real-life situations (Blueprints for Healthy Youth Development, 2018).

Although there are lesson objectives and scripts for teachers to follow, there is flexibility built into the program that allows teachers to adapt the lessons to address their particular classroom need (Blueprints for Healthy Youth Development, 2018). Parents are provided with information and activities that they may choose to review and complete with their students (Capp et al., 2017).

In addition to the five conceptual domains, there are five conceptual models that provide the foundational basis for PATHS and are used together with the program to ensure that the program is comprehensive, developmentally appropriate, and addresses students' cognition, emotion, and behavior (Blueprints for Healthy Youth Development, 2018).

- **Affective-Behavioral-Cognitive-Dynamic (ABCD)**: focuses on the promotion of developmental growth for each student and informs appropriate skill building and integration of affect with emotion, language, behavior, and cognitive understanding to promote social and emotional competence.
- **Eco-Behavioral System Orientation**: emphasizes the manner in which teachers use the curriculum model and generalize the skills to build a healthy classroom atmosphere to support students' use of the learned material.
- **Neurobiology and Brain Organization**: strategies to maximize the nature and quality of teacher-student and student-student interactions that impact brain development and learning.
- **Developmental Psychodynamic Theory and Education**: aims to coordinate social, emotional, and cognitive growth.
- **Psychological Concepts of Emotional Awareness (or emotional intelligence)**: Central to PATHS programming is the encouragement of students to discuss their feelings, experiences, opinions, and needs that are personally meaningful. Through these conversations students will feel listened to, supported, and respected by both their teachers and peers. The internal feelings of being valued, cared for, and appreciated motivate students to value, care for, and appreciate not only themselves, but their environment, their social groups, other people, and their world (Capp et al., 2017; Blueprints for Healthy Youth Development, 2018).

As a result of participating in the PATHS program, schools have seen a decrease in aggressive behavior, conduct problems, violent responses to social problems, delinquency and anxiety/depression (Capp, 2017; National Gang Center, 2018). Several studies on the effectiveness of PATHS indicate significant improvements in students' academics, self-control, frustration tolerance, conflict-resolution strategies, improved thinking and planning skills, and understanding and recognition of emotion (Capp et al., 2017; National Gang Center, 2018; Blueprint for Healthy Youth Development, 2018).

Olweus Bullying Prevention Program (OBPP)

The Olweus Bullying Prevention Program is another school-wide, multi-level, and multi-component comprehensive program based on a systematic restructuring of a school's environment and designed to reduce and prevent bullying in grades 1 through 9 (Blueprints for Healthy Youth Development, 2018). The program's framework is based on the development and modification of aggressive behavior and positive child-rearing dimensions and aims to redirect bullying behavior and reward prosocial behaviors (Capp et al., 2017).

OBPP is designed to improve student relationships with each other and make the school a safer, healthier, and more positive environment that fosters student learning and development (Capp et al., 2017). The goal of the program is to reduce existing amounts of bullying while preventing new bullying issues by structuring the school in such a way that teachers are engaged, caring, able to set limits regarding unacceptable behavior, willing to provide negative consequences for violence, and are able to exert authority and serve as positive role models (Capp et al., 2017).

The OBPP includes school level, classroom level, community, and individual level components (Blueprint for Healthy Youth Development, 2018). School level components include establishing a Bullying Prevention Coordinating Committee that is responsible for trainings on the program as well as administering a questionnaire that assesses the prevalence of existing bullying (Blueprints for a Healthy Youth Development, 2018).

In addition to introducing the school rules against bullying, the committee reviews any existing system or develops a system that will ensure supervision of students outside the classroom (Blueprints for Healthy Youth Development, 2018). Schools may wish to hold a kick-off event to launch the program and involve local community and parent participation (Capp et al., 2017).

Classroom components include regular class meetings to discuss and participate in activities that define and enforce rules against bullying as well as reinforce anti-bullying values and norms (Blueprints for Healthy Youth Development, 2018). The program also encourages and supports parental involvement through meetings and discussions on school violence and the efforts being made by the school to address it (Blueprints for Healthy Youth Development, 2018).

Individual components include personalized interventions with students who have a history of bullying and/or victimization, victims, and parents, and are designed to ensure cessation of violent behavior and provide support to its victims (Blueprints for Healthy Youth Development, 2018). Student activities should be supervised by an OBPP trained educator who is capable and willing to intervene immediately when any bullying occurs (Capp et al., 2017).

At the community level, partnerships should be developed, and community members should sit on the prevention committee to support the program within their local schools and help disseminate anti-bullying messages and principles of best practice (Capp et al., 2017). Through the involvement of school principals, teachers, students, parents, and the greater community in all components of the program, rules can be collaboratively enforced and bullying actively discouraged (Capp et al., 2017; Blueprints for Healthy Youth Development, 2018).

Schools across the world who have implemented this program have reported a significant reduction of bullying, victimization, delinquency, fighting, vandalism, truancy, and theft (Capp et al., 2017). Students themselves have reported improved order and discipline, better attitudes toward school and schoolwork, and more positive social relationships (Capp et al., 2017; Blueprints for Healthy Youth Development, 2018). Research into results of the program also indicate greater support for students who are bullied, and stronger, more effective interventions for students who bully others (Capp et al., 2017).

Positive Behavioral Interventions and Supports (PBIS)

The Positive Behavioral Interventions and Supports model, as named directly in the 1997 reauthorization of the Individuals with Disabilities Education Act (IDEA), is a comprehensive, proactive, whole-school intervention used by more than 20,000 schools (Capp et al., 2017). To create safe and supporting learning environments for all students, PBIS is designed to involve the entire school population in the creation of a positive school environment, promote student success through rewarding behaviors, while preventing and/or reducing negative, risky, and/or problem behaviors in elementary, middle, and high schools (Barrett, Eber, & Weist, n.d.; Freeman et al., 2018; Towvim et al., 2012).

To implement PBIS in schools requires a system-wide change that encompasses seven major components:

1. an agreed upon common approach to discipline;
2. a positive statement of purpose;
3. positive expectations for all students and staff;
4. procedures to teach students the expectations;
5. procedures to encourage and sustain the expectations;
6. procedures to discourage rule-violating behavior; and
7. procedures to regularly and frequently monitor and evaluate the discipline system. (Barrett et al., n.d.; PBIS, 2018)

The PBIS framework enables and assists school personnel to adopt and organize evidence-based behavioral interventions into an integrated continuum that seeks to enhance academic and social behavior outcomes for all students (PBIS, 2018; Simonsen & Freeman, 2018).

Unlike other school safety and violence prevention programs, PBIS does not have a set curriculum, scripted intervention, or manualized strategy. Instead, PBIS is a prevention-oriented method with the same logic, tenets, and principles as response to intervention (RTI) strategies, which allow administrators and educators to organize evidence-based practices, improve implementation of those practices, and maximize academic and social behavior outcomes for all students (PBIS, 2018; Simonsen & Freeman, 2018).

PBIS emphasizes that organizational systems should be established at the school, district, and state levels, to give school personnel the capacity to utilize effective interventions accurately and successfully (PBIS, 2018). Systems of support should include team-based leadership, data-based decision-making, continuous monitoring of student behavior, regular universal screening, and effective ongoing professional development (PBIS, 2018).

The PBIS program consists of teaching, modeling, and reinforcing prosocial or desired behaviors utilizing three levels of intervention within each school (Barrett et al., n.d.). Primary interventions include teaching, modeling, and reinforcing prosocial behavior and expectations for all students through, for example, a school-wide token system (PBIS, 2018). Secondary level interventions are intended for specific school settings, such as a cafeteria or hallway, or for students who are continually at risk for problem behaviors and can include small group counseling (Simonsen & Freeman, 2018) The third level of interventions are individualized for students with chronic behavioral problems and include specific plans such as school-based mental health services (Capp et al., 2017).

The opinions and perspectives of family and local community members are included in the PBIS process through active participation on leadership teams, in practice implementation, and in outcome evaluations at the school, district, and state levels (Simonsen & Freeman, 2018). By tailoring PBIS to local strengths and needs, PBIS can be integrated with other programming, such as alcohol and drug prevention and social-emotional learning programs (Towvim et al., 2012).

Although PBIS has no specific restrictions on the use of consequence-based strategies designed to reduce school violence, teaching-oriented, positive, and preventive strategies are emphasized for all students to address even the most severe behaviors (PBIS, 2018). PBIS supports teachers in changing their behavior to positively influence and interact with students and in helping them create, communicate, and enforce behavioral expectations for all students, provide feedback, mitigate and respond to problem behaviors, and improve interactions among students and staff (PBIS, 2018).

Research has demonstrated that the implementation of a PBIS model school-wide, with ongoing data collection, progress monitoring, problem solving, and effective decision-making regarding behavioral challenges, is effective for increasing feelings of school safety and reducing problem behaviors and violence in schools (Capp et al., 2017; Simonsen & Freeman, 2018; PBIS, 2018). PBIS implementation has resulted in increases in prosocial behavior, a healthy school climate, and better academic outcomes including increased test scores, and decreases in discipline referrals, suspensions, and bullying (Towvim et al., 2012; Barrett et al., n.d.; PBIS, 2018). Empirical evidence has also shown that the implementation of PBIS resulted in the decreased use of crisis procedures in alternative education settings (Simonsen & Freeman, 2018).

When immersed in a positive school culture where informative corrective feedback is provided, academic success is maximized, and the use of prosocial skills is acknowledged, most students will succeed (PBIS, 2018). When problematic behavior is unresponsive to preventive school and classroom procedures, feedback about the student's behavior is used to understand why the problem behavior occurred, strengthen acceptable alternative behaviors, remove precursors and consequences that cause and maintain problem behavior, and add precursors and consequences that trigger and maintain acceptable alternative behaviors (PBIS, 2018).

SUCCESSFUL INTERVENTIONS

Successful school-wide interventions that address school violence and safety share core characteristics in that they are comprehensive interventions enacted throughout all levels of a school, raise awareness, investment, and responsibility from students, teachers, and parents, and establish clear expectations and rules for the whole school (Capp et al., 2017; Pitner, Marachi, Astor, & Benbenishty, 2015).

Interventions seek to increase supervision and monitoring outside of the classroom, use faculty, staff, and parents to plan, implement and sustain the intervention, and create clear expectations and procedures before, during, and after incidences of violence (Pitner et al., 2015). Successful programs all include continuous monitoring so that schools may tailor interventions to their own unique environments and increase the potential for success (Capp et al., 2017; Pitner et al., 2015).

SYSTEMATIC MONITORING

One of the most important and essential elements for interventions to remain successful and continuously improve, is the ongoing and interactive use of data. Collected data should be used to build awareness, assess the extent of school violence, plan and implement interventions, and conduct evaluations (Capp et al., 2017; Pitner et al., 2015). In addition, school-specific data should be shared consistently with administrators, educators, parents, and the greater community throughout the assessment and implementation periods so schools can identify their needs, strengths, resources, and limitations (Capp et al., 2017; Pitner et al., 2015).

Using Monitoring to Address School Violence and School Safety

Research from countries such as the United States, Israel, and France, has demonstrated how systematic monitoring has been used to collect and interpret data from multiple layers within a school to quantify and explore concerning issues within schools (Capp et al., 2017). In the United States, for example, 145 schools used monitoring data to identify areas of concern such as bullying, school safety, weapon use, and substance use (Capp et al., 2017).

Once the data was collected and reviewed and each school's individual needs were determined, evidence-based practices and interventions were chosen for implementation in the school (Capp et al., 2017). Among those interventions that were chosen and implemented were the OBPP, Second Step, Student-to-Student, Safe School Ambassadors, and Cognitive Behavioral Intervention for Trauma in Schools (CBITS) (Capp et al., 2017).

FINAL THOUGHTS

Successful school-wide interventions that address school violence and safety through clear expectations and rules for all levels of a school can raise awareness, elicit investment, and promote responsibility among students, teachers, parents, and the local community.

Interventions must be sustained by faculty, staff, and parents and provide for continuous monitoring so that schools may constantly tailor the interventions to their own unique school environments, thereby increasing the potential for their success. Research consistently demonstrates that school violence is preventable through the reduction of risk factors and the promotion of protective factors at the individual, relational, community, and societal level.

Teaching and modeling positive behaviors to all students leads to an encouraging, supportive school climate in which students feel connected, learning is promoted, and negative behaviors are reduced. Schools that participate in prevention and safety programs have seen decreases in aggressive behavior, conduct problems, and violent responses to social problems in addition to improvements in students' academics, self-control, frustration tolerance, and conflict-resolution strategies.

POINTS TO REMEMBER

- *Students' experiences, knowledge, and skills are predictors of their future involvement in violence; therefore, the development of positive relationships between students and their peers, teachers, and families is critical to their well-being and preventing school violence.*
- *When planning interventions strategies and implementing violence prevention programs, every school must consider its own unique sociocultural influences, school climate, the nature of its problems and their severity.*
- *The Promoting Alternative Thinking Strategies (PATHS) program is one of the highest-rated social-emotional learning and violence prevention programs due to its ability to reduce aggression, promote social and emotional competence, and enhance the educational process.*
- *The Olweus Bullying Prevention Program's (OBPP) ability to redirect bullying behavior and reward prosocial behaviors has resulted in a significant reduction of bullying, victimization, delinquency, and fighting among students in school.*
- *Positive Behavioral Intervention and Support (PBIS) programs can be tailored to a school's strengths and needs as well as integrated with other preventative programming, such as alcohol and drug prevention and social-emotional learning programs. Implementation of PBIS can result in increased prosocial behavior, a healthy school climate, and better academic outcomes such as increased test scores.*

Chapter 6

Creating the Peaceable Kingdom
Cultivating Student Well-Being and Connectedness

While some solutions to school safety obviously lie at the national, political level, others are located within schools themselves, in the mental health system, and in families and communities themselves. In the search for solutions, some common strategies emerge, clustered in a number of identifiable domains and inextricably linked to best practices in school, family, and community health and well-being. In addressing the topics of violence prevention, reduction, and schools as safe havens for cognitive, social, and emotional development, using components of "the peaceable kingdom," in which all students can grow and thrive, offers some possible solutions to very difficult issues.

The painter Edward Hicks created many versions of his masterpiece, The Peaceable Kingdom. Derived from the Book of Isaiah, 11:6-8, it recounts the following Biblical verse:

The wolf did with the lambkin dwell in peace
His grim carnivorous nature there did cease
The leopard with the harmless kid laid down
And not one savage beast was seen to frown.
The lion with the fatling on did move
A little child was leading them in love.

The notion of enemies in the animal world mingling in peace together spurs a powerful image of what could happen in our nation's schools if they were bastions of mental and emotional health, well-being, respect, and true community. Schools are rethinking and reimagining their culture and curriculum in the hopes that such peace and tranquility can replace episodes of victimization, division, isolation, and violence.

COMPONENTS OF THE PEACEABLE KINGDOM

The peaceable school is constructed of several components to include school connectedness, positive discipline, relational education, mental health and well-being, and respect for diversity (Page, 2017; Calderon, 2017; Fronius et al., 2016; McMahon, 2016). These spill over into different fields—education, psychology, human growth and development, academic engagement, parent and community engagement, and mental health; yet they share vital ties as each component

- is critical to building an environment that meets students' needs for belonging, recognition and positive regard in a way that lessens the possibilities of acting out in ways that are harmful to self and others.
- works holistically with the others to create an environment and school culture that nurtures all members of the learning community while helping them discover who they are as unique individuals, what they love most and excel at, and how they can assist others in reaching their innate potential.
- raises awareness in cases in which behaviors that are warning signs or cries for help are more likely to be noticed and receive appropriate attention before they escalate.

CULTIVATING POSITIVE EMOTIONAL HEALTH AND WELL-BEING

The majority of people with poor mental health do not commit violent acts; yet it bears mentioning that positive health and well-being among all members of a school community lessen the likelihood of actions that result in all levels of violence—from bullying and microaggressions to escalated levels of violence against others, to disengagement, depression, and self-harm (Safe and Sounds Schools, 2016).

Page (2017) underscores five major components of building better mental health in schools to include (1) integrated discussions surrounding mental health and school curriculum, (2) school as a safe learning environment, (3) the well-being of the entire school to include staff, (4) ensure that staff knows how to help in time of need, and (5) the knowledge that this endeavor requires the help of students, staff, families, and the community.

Discussions surrounding the mental health needs of students requires integration into the school curriculum and normalization so that stigmas of mental health and self-identification of potential issues will be removed (Page, 2017). In many cases, students feel a sense of shame if they recognize problems or stressors that they cannot handle sufficiently; in other cases, students simply may not have the information that they need to identify issues in themselves or in their friends. Knowledge and acceptance are key elements of a healthy school environment and these elements increase the likelihood that psychological and emotional issues can be addressed before they escalate (Page, 2017).

Schools should strive to be a true safe haven for everyone in the learning community and meet the most basic of Maslow's (1987) hierarchy of needs by providing nutrition, protection of mind and body and a safe and healthy school environment in terms of buildings and grounds; however, it also must address higher needs, such as love, belonging, and acceptance, as well as esteem, self-confidence, achievement and respect (Page, 2017). Without those, what is deemed to be the purpose of education, and the foundation of prosocial health and well-being (self-actualization) cannot occur fully.

The necessity of good peer and teacher relationships, feeling listened to and "heard" when concerns are raised and being a valued member of the school community are critical counters to the disengagement that may result in antisocial or self-harming behaviors (Page, 2017). Well-being is not merely a student issue, rather, it is a whole-school concern and addressing the well-being of staff makes it more likely that they will have the focus and energy to address student needs (Kaufman, 2013; Page, 2017).

The research of Wyn, Cahill, Holdsworth, Rowling, & Carson (2000) showed that mental health training assisted staff in bolstering their own resilience and job satisfaction. Using a program of national mental health promotion, Australia was able to facilitate best practices in the promotion of school-wide mental health and well-being, while teaching protocol and interventions that could be used with a wide variety of issues in school (Wyn et al., 2000). The program also aimed to develop partnerships among schools, families and community agencies through the dissemination of this program (Wyn et al., 2000).

What Wyn et al. (2000) discovered was that when educators were comfortable and competent in teaching for mental health and creating classroom and school environments that nurtured prosocial behaviors, their own stress and anxiety decreased, and they were able to consider aspects of their own well-being from a different perspective. Adopting a whole-school initiative allowed for a common language and set of procedures for everyone to follow, thus lessening the burden on any individual in the school community if faced with challenges and stressors. Schools with higher levels of positive mental health among all constituents also decrease the kinds of adult bullying and violence mentioned in previous chapters.

The MindMatters program (n.d.) takes a whole-school approach of creating an ethos of mental health, even though only about 20–30 percent of any school's students may need additional psychosocial intervention, and 3–12 percent may need additional mental health intervention in the form of professional treatment outside of school (Wyn et al., 2000). All students and staff require cognate knowledge, attitudes, and awareness of the ways to promote resiliency, reduce stress, and recognize when symptoms suggest the need for additional support; thus, the model begins with an individualized audit and then tailors professional development based upon what schools establish as their own priorities for whole-school action (MindMatters, n.d.).

Each school should assess the knowledge base of new hires in relation to key training, such as their understanding of risk and resilience factors for their students, how to recognize signs of different mental health illnesses, how to support students in crisis, and when and how to seek additional help, including a clear knowledge of the protocol and policies in place in their school (Page, 2017). Gaps in any of these areas can be addressed through individualized education to bring new teachers and staff up to speed.

National Alliance on Mental Illness (NAMI) (2018) offers a program for educators and parents, to give information necessary to become aware, effective allies for children, using an initial information session that builds public and parental knowledge regarding "the warning signs of mental health conditions and what steps to take if you or a loved one are showing symptoms of a mental illness" (NAMI, 2018, n.p.).

Rahim (2015) summarizes the necessary stance of schools in promoting an open dialogue about mental health in developmentallyappropriate ways across the school years. Each school must be willing to find ways to share three messages.

- *"It's ok to talk about mental illness"* (Rahim, 2015, n.p.): This statement effectively ends the taboo on this delicate topic.
- *"There is no shame in seeking help"* (Rahim, 2015, n.p.): This statement encourages students to make their needs known in order to receive appropriate diagnosis and treatment.
- *"There is hope after the diagnosis"* (Rahim, 2015, n.p.): This message touts the positive outcomes of appropriate treatment and the possibility of "normalcy" that is so desperately sought by children and adolescents.

Rahim (2015) further outlines concrete strategies from incorporating these messages into the everyday life of a school urging schools to provide accurate information about mental illness that avoids negative attitudes and stresses that it can affect anyone and is not the result of bad character, upbringing, or personal traits. There needs to be opportunities to actually have dialogues about the conditions and how to talk with people about mental illness;

effectively demonstrating that it is acceptable to bring this topic into the open can range from awareness programs, lunchtime safe spaces, bringing in guest speakers, and having clear safety protocols in place (Rahim, 2015).

If students are ashamed of their mental health challenges, they are apt to disengage or go underground with their thoughts and feelings; thus, all students and staff need to be informed of the available resources so that if they need them, or if a friend or peer confides in them or shares troubling thoughts or emotions, they are prepared to act (Rahim, 2015). Students are unlikely to confide in others unless the school is permeated by an attitude of acceptance and simple approaches such as active, nonjudgmental listening, compassion, normalizing fears and negative emotions and seeking help as a positive action (Rahim, 2015).

As students get older, they tend to feel that they should be able to deal with issues themselves; especially males, who may feel greater stigma in accessing mental health counseling (Page, 2017). One of the most effective ways to reach adolescents is through programming that uses celebrities and well-known or familiar figures with mental health conditions to talk about their own experiences and outcomes. This is part of the way to assure students that there is, indeed, life after a mental health diagnosis.

Page (2017) also mentions the value of programming to build resilience and alleviate social isolation to include extracurricular social activities, peer and adult mentoring, and service activities can build esteem while modeling prosocial behaviors.

STUDENT ENGAGEMENT

In summarizing the latest Gallup Student Engagement Poll, Calderon (2017) articulates seminal information about the engagement needs of students over various grade levels. In response to the survey, students identified nine engagement items that were critical to their academic and social success, as well as their sense of school safety and belonging to include:

1. At this school, I get to do what I do best every day.
2. My teachers make me feel my schoolwork is important.
3. I feel safe in this school.
4. I have fun at school.
5. I have a best friend at school.
6. In the last seven days, someone has told me I have done good work at school.
7. In the last seven days, I have learned something interesting at school.

8. The adults at my school care about me.
9. I have at least one teacher who makes me excited about the future. (Calderon, 2017)

The most disappointing news about student engagement is that it wanes as students' progress in age and grade in school; however, there are many ways in which educators can reverse this trend, starting with implanting a sense of personal hope for the future in each student (Calderon, 2017).

Effective teachers devote real time to helping students formulate dreams for the future, getting them to articulate pragmatic steps for reaching them, and then instilling in their charges the necessary habits, academic knowledge and hands-on skills to arrive at their destination (Calderon, 2017). This entails identifying and nurturing individual students' assets and gifts as they are more likely to be goal oriented when given genuine support and recognition from others they admire. In the pursuit of inspired schools, administration needs to give greater recognition to those teachers and staff who create safe, supportive environments that allow young dreamers to flourish (Calderon, 2017).

CONNECTEDNESS

One of the clearest ways to create peaceable schools is through positive student-teacher relationships. Strong, consistent, caring teacher-student relationships promote students' social and academic skills, and these, in turn, lessen the chances of behavioral infractions (O'Connor, Dearing, & Collins, 2011). When teachers build classroom environments that lend positive social and emotional support to students, those classrooms can become safe spaces where students can take part in socially productive learning and behaviors (O'Connor et al., 2011).

Students also learn about social norms and behavioral expectations in this way; therefore, their actions and values are consonant with school expectations and beliefs (O'Connor et al., 2011). Students who are living in poverty or of a low socioeconomic status particularly need these positive student-teacher relationships and positive behavioral programs; however, all students need to be educated in a classroom culture of respect, relationships with others, and inclusion (Jensen, 2009).

Connection in schools is derived, in large part, from what has been called "relational teaching" (Gibbs, 2015, p. 1). In a study in Great Britain, the power of relational teaching was revealed

> In comparing schools, the team found that those they classified as relatively "relational" not only helped students achieve better academic outcomes, but also brought a wider range of additional benefits too. Critically, in schools with

better relational qualities, students' relationships with both their peers and their teachers improved as the young people progressed through the school, with a notable decline in bullying levels. These effects are even greater where a school is intentional about building relationships; levels of well-being are higher, bullying levels and absences are lower, and physical health is improved. In one case, a school—described as like a "family" by students—was considered by social services as one of the best environments in the region for looked-after children (Gibbs, 2015, p. 1).

This same finding is reported in a New Harbinger (2015) report. In it, the work of researchers Reichert and Hawley (2013) is explicated; the two set out to study relational teaching approaches as a means to shrink the gap between the achievement levels of boys and girls, particularly boys of color. Teachers who understood and cultivated valuable relationships with their students took responsibility for maintaining a working alliance with their students and they believed it was their role to serve as an expert learning guide, maintain an awareness of the quality of the relationship and work to repair or address any strains in that relationship (Reichert & Hawley, 2013).

Beyond maintaining high standards and demonstrating mastery of their subject expertise, relational teachers did other things that aided student achievement to include

- Reaching out to improvise measures to meet a particular student's needs,
- Responding to a student's personal interest or talent,
- Sharing a common interest with students, and
- Refusing to personalize oppositional behavior and responding with civility and restraint until the student came around. (Reichert & Hawley, 2013)

These helped interpersonal bonds form that then allowed for the modeling of prosocial behavior (New Harbinger, 2015). With greater connection, there was a decrease in acting out behavior and more time and attention devoted to closing the achievement gap (New Harbinger, 2015).

While Reichert and Hawley (2013) were specifically concerned with male academic performance, other studies have shown that while girls outstrip boys in nearly all measures of academic success, they have higher levels of psychological stress, stronger reactions to stress, and higher rates of depression, eating disorders, and other mental health disorders. A recent study by Liang and Spencer (2013) looked at the unique challenges facing adolescent girls. One of the most salient findings was that close relationships with significant others was directly related to higher levels of female well-being (Liang & Spencer, 2013). This indicates that both genders can reap benefits from relational teaching and other forms of social connection in school.

POSITIVE DISCIPLINE

When one Baltimore school replaced detention with alternative forms of intervention, not one detention was reported in an entire year (Haupt, 2016; Allen, 2018). There is a growing movement to consider different forms of discipline that reduce incidents of behavior problems, teach valuable life skills, and address what issues there are in ways that preserve student dignity and keep them integrated into the positive school culture (Owen, Wettach, & Hoffman, 2015).

Positive Behavioral Interventions and Supports, more often called PBIS (2018), is a disciplinary system being used in a variety of U.S. schools that aims to minimize student behavioral infractions through the use of systematic strategies that are consonant with each individual school's behavioral expectations and targeted interventions. Undergirding the system are cultural and social approaches to behavior interventions; the PBIS system is founded on interventions and strategies that focus on changing the context in which problematic behavior occurs (Positive Behavioral Interventions & Supports [PBIS], 2018; Bosworth & Judkins, 2014).

PBIS was developed to build school cultures and climates in which it is not socially acceptable for students to act out in negative ways. It is a collaborative approach that involves teachers, students, school administration, parents, and community members in a systematic approach to behavioral interventions (Martin, 2013). Created with three levels, the program makes the first and primary level a school-wide application; the second level is that of the classroom, followed by the third—the individual.

The approach relies on multiple behavior supports such as specific behavioral plans, reward systems, and point sheets for students ranging from classroom settings to hallways, restrooms, and buses (Martin, 2013). Beginning with the earliest grades, schools teach and reinforce common behavioral expectations so that students have no doubt about what the school norms are. If inappropriate behavior does occur, the entire school community can act rapidly and consistently, creating a sense of stability in the interactions of all school community members (Martin, 2013).

PBIS addresses how students are treated by teachers and school staff members using tiered instruction and concentrates on the awareness of staff and students of behavioral data such as the current suspension rate as compared to past years (PBIS, 2018). PBIS also focuses on classroom-based behavioral and social instruction for all students and school staff (Bosworth & Judkins, 2014).

Consistency and equity are the key components of PBIS, so it is required that all teachers and administrators use similar behavioral terminology and their expectations for student behavioral norms do not deviate among individuals or groups (PBIS, 2018). Consistency does not occur in a vacuum, so there must be didactic experiences and constant modeling of desired norms. This consistency then establishes a school culture in which everyone knows what expectations are in different situations to include the lunch room, classroom, assembly, sports event or security drill, as examples (Martin, 2013). With these norms established and practiced, teachers and staff can spend more time on positive actions such as classroom instruction, building a school climate, service to community, or other worthwhile activities (PBIS, 2018).

Beegle (2009) compiled a list of best practices for educating students from generational poverty that corroborates the seminal philosophy of the PBIS approach. Both Beegle's (2009) list and PBIS (2018) strategies include developing strong teacher-student relationships, holding high behavioral expectations for all students, being able to articulate these expectations clearly, training all school staff, and setting up mentoring programs.

PBIS can be a tool for transforming school culture and climate when it is effectively woven into the fabric of an institution that prizes positive approaches to relationships, behavior, and tolerance for diversity (Lewis & Sugai, 2008). A school's culture has the greatest effect on levels of school violence and a positive school culture cannot exist without genuine collaboration among all members (Waters & Marzano, 2006).

RESTORATIVE JUSTICE

Restorative justice (RJ) is described as dealing with disciplinary incidents by identifying and implementing the means for perpetrators of violence to repair the damage resulting by their choices and behaviors (Wachtel, 2016). There are three primary levels of stakeholders according to the restorative justice philosophy: victims, offenders, and the greater community, which in education is identified as the school culture and the student body (Wachtel, 2016). All stakeholders will hold needs that may be emotional, social, and logistical (Wachtel, 2016).

In the emotional domain, a victim might need to hear an apology or understand, through the perpetrator's explanation, why a particular act of violence was chosen (Wachtel, 2016). In the social sphere, the perpetrator needs to understand the community's perceptions about how the act of violence has affected them (Wachtel, 2016). Logistical needs are expressed in an articulation of how a student who might have damaged a school building or playground intends to repair these damages and make the appropriate reparations (Wachtel, 2016).

Within mediation, sometimes called a restorative conference, the two parties must come together in a carefully scripted dialogue to talk. This means of dealing with violence forces both parties to interact in supervised settings and relies on the expressions from each side as means of coming to greater understanding, as well as reparation of damages (Wachtel, 2016).

While there has not been a long history of research on restorative justice programs, a study conducted in 2009 on a restorative justice program in low socio-economic status (SES) schools proved promising (Lewis, 2009). At the time of the study, one school in particular, West Philadelphia High School, had just begun the restorative justice program, yet a short time after implementation, a 52 percent drop in violent acts and serious incidents was noted from the 2006–2007 school year to the 2007–2008 school year (Lewis, 2009).

Student offenders with a single disciplinary infraction that would have warranted their suspension was reduced from 246 during the 2006–2007 school year to 188 during the 2007–2008 school year and those with multiple disciplinary infractions that would have warranted a suspension in the past decreased from 264 students in 2006–2007 to 200 students during the 2007–2008 school year (Lewis, 2009).

The most comprehensive study of restorative justice to date, reviewed research on schools across the United States using similar programs and pointed out the need for clearer and more consistent definitions of "restorative justice" before too many conclusions about its efficacy could be reached (Fronius, 2016). Fronius et al. (2016), however, did find that "preliminary evidence does suggest that RJ [restorative justice] may have positive effects across several outcomes related to discipline, attendance and graduation, climate and culture, and various academic outcomes" (p. 26).

The efficacy of restorative justice in developing and nurturing a positive school culture and climate remains small, yet there are some recent studies and reviews that seem positive (Ortega, Lyubansky, Nettles, & Espelage, 2016; Fronius et al., 2016). Ortega et al. (2016) conducted a study using semi-structured interviews involving administrators, staff, and students at the high school level.

The research revealed perceptions that there were many positive effects of restorative justice on school culture because students and administration and staff arrived at an increased level of understanding of the disciplinary process, why student disciplinary infractions occurred, how these infractions could be avoided in the future, and how to use meaningful dialogue when there was a problem, or a student had broken a school rule (Ortega et al., 2016). In short, students and staff believed that restorative justice had a positive effect on school culture and climate (Ortega et al., 2016).

ALTERNATIVE FORMS OF DISCIPLINE

Some of the more fascinating approaches to discipline—with an eye toward teaching all students self-regulation skills, while avoiding punishments and missed school time through detention or suspension—involve alternative approaches derived from yoga, meditation, and mindfulness (Lewis, 2009; Fronius et al., 2016). While initially scoffed at, these programs are gathering empirical data, besides just the anecdotal, to mount support for their infusion in all public schools.

One case study that has garnered national attention is at Robert W. Coleman Elementary School in West Baltimore. As the reporter did a feature story on the discipline program, an enraged student was sent to the meditation room after a name-calling incident escalated into a physical altercation (Bloom, 2016). "I did some deep breathing, had a little snack, and I got myself together," the boy recalled, "Then I apologized to my class" (Bloom, 2016, p. 1). The Mindful Movement Room, as it is called, contains throw pillows, yoga mats, and soothing scents; in it, students can stretch, calm down, do yoga, or meditate or do deep breathing, all ways to restore peace in the individuals and the classroom or school yard (St. George, 2016).

Mindfulness continues as staff members talk with students sent to the room, discussing their infractions and launching them into deep breathing (St. George, 2016). Given the school's population—which hails from homeless shelters, impoverished and violent neighborhoods—this is a new strategy to address students' troubles and teach them strategies for future use (Bloom, 2016).

All students at the school begin and end their school days with fifteen minutes of guided meditation; they can practice yoga during and after school. Bloom (2016) cites a Journal of American Medical Association Internal Medicine's 2014 study revealing that mindfulness meditation helps to alleviate anxiety, depression, and pain. Simply learning that each action doesn't need to be met with a reaction allows students to make more thoughtful and peaceful choices.

McMahon (2016) reports on other projects that include a whole child, socio-emotional learning approach. In Minnesota, teachers work with the Mindfulness in Schools Project (n.d.) that helps teach students to manage classroom distractions that detract from their learning. In one school, all students meditate quietly at the beginning and end of each class, both to focus on the learning ahead and calm themselves before classroom exchanges, where much of any school's disruptions occur (Davis, 2016).

Syracuse (NY) schools, by order of the state attorney general, have moved from disciplinary actions to using behavioral practices like those mentioned previously; these actions came as a result of learning that students of color in the Syracuse City School District were twice as likely to be suspended long term as were white students (Simidian, 2017). All of these are steps toward a less punitive view of school discipline to one that is more restorative.

Yoga 4 Classrooms, in conjunction with the University of Massachusetts (Lowell) and Brigham and Woman's Hospital (Harvard Medical School) conducted a research study on cortisol and behavior in second and third grade students to determine if there were effects from a classroom yoga and meditation program on their physiological stress, perceived behavior, and attention (Ebert & Flynn, 2014). These practices appeared to have salutary effects on the children, leading to questions about other applications. In general, however, the students showed a decrease in cortisol levels and improvements in creativity, ability to control their behavior, and ability to manage anger (Ebert & Flynn, 2014).

Paying attention to social-emotional learning is critical. Within the human brain lies the amygdala, a structure that is often called the alarm system of the brain because of its involvement in emotional responses (Banks & Hirschman, 2016). When the amygdala is activated, it becomes very difficult for students to engage in new learning or concentration because the cortical memory systems retrieve and prioritize information relevant to the current, perceived stressful situation rather than cognitively processing new learning (Wolfe, 2010).

Teaching with the emotions in mind creates a positive learning environment for students; therefore, lessening or sidetracking reactions in the alarm system altogether (Jensen, 2009). Mindfulness meditation can lower perceived threats, calming a student's system so that s/he can avoid triggering alert systems and potentially mistaking threats or overreacting.

Interestingly, another value of these alternative approaches to behavior management and discipline may lie in teacher well-being. One third of all newly hired teachers either resign or report burning out in their first three to five years of teaching and nearly 70 percent of K-12 teachers say they are not engaged in their work, while 9 percent suffer from major depressive symptoms (Ebert & Flynn, 2014; Gallup, 2014).

Given this state of affairs, teacher well-being is likely to have an effect on their perceptions of and reactions to student behavior. Not only have recent studies found that yoga and mindfulness meditation are beneficial to teachers' health, lowering their stress levels and returning more joy to their work, but once having experienced their benefits, teachers are more interested in integrating the techniques into their own classrooms (Kamenetz, 2016).

ATTENDING TO GENDER VARIABLES

Quinn (2013) notes that the educational experiences of male and female students can be very different. While many believe that contemporary pedagogy still continues to alienate and silence female students and that girls are expected to be more rule-conforming than boys, there lacks a robust body of research to back this up. Overall, girls tend to achieve at a higher academic rate in terms of grade-point average than male students, but there are greater expectations for good behavior, neatness, and help-giving in class that hamper girls' expression (Quinn, 2013).

Despite all of the emphasis on enticing more female students into the STEM areas, there still is greater acceptance for girls to go into traditionally female-dominated professions such as nursing and teaching (Miller et al., 2015). When students are at a social disadvantage due to stereotyped teacher expectation, classrooms can become psychologically and emotionally threatening places; this social disadvantage may result in behavioral infractions (Miller et al., 2015).

Historically, researchers have found that female students have fewer opportunities than boys to engage in classroom discussions, demonstrate their knowledge in front of the class, and answer questions posed by the teacher (Huang, 2014). Teachers are more likely to expect female students to be passive and quiet while their male counterparts are expected to be active and talkative and are afforded the space and freedom in classrooms to do so (Huang, 2014).

In both small-group discussions and whole-class activities, teachers often gave preference to the opinions of boys over girls; males more frequently interrupted female students when they attempted to speak; and teachers often assigned tasks such as taking notes during class discussions to female students, rather than encouraging them to be active and voice their opinions (Huang, 2014).

Often, behavioral infractions were addressed differently according to one's gender, with teachers, staff, and administration tending to mete out more punitive and severe consequences, such as classroom removals and office referrals, to girls when compared to the punishments that male students receive for the same types of behavior in the classroom (Huang, 2014).

In the mid-1990s into the turn of the century, there was a great deal of emphasis on the unfair treatment that girls received in school classrooms and other settings yet, simultaneously, research was released that demonstrated that schools were unfair to male students in the severity of punishments given to them when compared to their female counterparts (Sommers, 2000; Buchmann, DiPrete, & McDaniel, 2008; AAUW, 1992; Sadker & Sadker, 1994).

Research by Pollack (1998, 2000) on "real boys" and "real boys' voices" illustrated that boys' express affection and loyalty in different forms from girls; these expressions often go unnoticed or are misunderstood or undervalued by elementary school teachers, who remain predominantly female. These same works demonstrated how socialization deprived boys of many avenues for emotional expression, leaving more physical and aggressive behaviors as ways of dealing with problems and feelings (Pollack, 1998, 2000).

Bertrand and Pan (2011) studied the behavioral skills of school children. Using data from over 20,000 students who entered kindergarten in 1998, including information on suspensions and expulsions, they followed these students until they exited eighth grade after the 2006–2007 school year (Bertrand & Pan, 2011).

After reviewing a wide variety of data in different behavioral domains, it was reported that female students committed fewer behavioral infractions in school than their male counterparts (Bertrand & Pan, 2011). When positive behavioral systems are implemented, school-wide behavioral expectations are consistent across genders; this can improve school culture because the same disciplinary protocols are in place for all (Mass-Galloway et al., 2008).

SOCIAL EMOTIONAL EDUCATION

Durlak, Weissberg, Dymnicki, Taylor, & Schellinger (2011) conducted a meta-analysis of social and emotional learning programs demonstrating that schools that had SEL programs achieved better academic results than those that did not. These skills can be taught in individual classrooms or school-wide and peer relationships and relationships with adults can be improved through didactic experiences that teach skills such as self and social-awareness, self-regulation, relational skills and responsible decision-making (CASEL, 2018).

Programs are most effective when they are active, focus on skill development, and have clear learning goals (Larmer, Mergendoller, & Boss, 2015; CASEL, 2018). The more that material can be delivered in ways that meet students' individual learning and cultural styles, the better (Celli & Young, 2014). Anxiety and aggression were also reduced through these programs (Durlak et al., 2011).

These programs are particularly important for students with disabilities who may not be skillful at reading body language, nuances, or behavioral norms (Durlak et al., 2011). It may be more difficult for such students to initiate relationships and to engage in the typical back and forth of social interchanges. Enhancing social and emotional skills is particularly important in these groups as they often are the target of victimization or may lose the ability to regulate their emotions and lash out at others (Durlak et al., 2011).

BUILDING STUDENTS' RESILIENCY

Repeated exposure to stress and risk may lead to some individuals developing psychopathologies, while exposure to toxic environments increases the risk of poverty, abuse, violence, and educational failure cycles (Henderson & Milstein, 2002). Stress can also overtax the amygdala whose primary job is to knit together emotional content and memory (Banks & Hirschman, 2016). When an individual undergoes a dangerous or stress-inducing situation, or one that is novel or unknown, this part of the brain becomes activated in order to concentrate on survival and, as such, it is not terribly open to receiving and comprehending new material; thus, learning is interrupted or blocked (Jensen, 2009; Banks & Hirschman, 2016).

Resiliency is the concept that humans can conquer stress and become stronger due to the process that they go through in overcoming stressors (Masten, 2018). Schools are vital to the positive academic and socio-emotional development of students because they can provide both the environment and the conditions that foster resiliency (Masten, 2018; Henderson & Milstein, 2002; Essex, 2012).

Educational personnel supervise students under their care and must ensure, to the best of their ability, that students feel that they are safe to take academic risks and explore both academically and socially (Essex, 2012). One of the main facets of building resilience in schools is that the school must be a place that provides care and support to all students (Henderson & Milstein, 2002). When students feel valued, listened to, and connected to others, they demonstrate ownership of their school in positive ways.

Henderson and Milstein (2002) proposed a profile of a resiliency-building school in the form of a circle in which one half is devoted to mitigating risk factors in a student's environment and the other in building resiliency. In reducing risk factors, the authors identify three mandates to include an increase in prosocial bonding, setting clear and consistent boundaries, and teaching "life skills."

Among these component pieces are such school qualities as a positive and supportive school culture, mentors and role models, equity, cooperative learning, involvement by all stakeholders in developing policies and rules, and risk-taking as skill development takes place (Henderson & Milstein, 2002). These are schools that are constantly striving to improve and that encourage students to learn not just the curriculum, but skills that will be transferable to their adult lives.

A number of qualities of resiliency-building schools are included on the other half of the wheel and target building a resilient school environment that includes providing meaningful opportunities for all students to contribute, setting and communicating high expectations, and providing care and support to all (Henderson & Milstein, 2002). Among these are that all individuals' contributions are seen as important, there is an atmosphere of cooperation and respect, experimentation is encouraged, and students are viewed as workers, with their teachers as the coaches (Henderson & Milstein, 2002).

Each student has his or her own individualized growth plan and students are encouraged to set high goals and not worry about failures along the way. Even small successes are celebrated, and all students have a sense of belonging. Leaders in resiliency-building schools spend a great amount of positive time with the school community members and a "can do" attitude pervades school problem solving (Henderson & Milstein, 2002).

As far back as the 1990s, Sagor (1996) conducted school development institutes on site to help schools identify ways that they could build resiliency in their students. A CBUPO (competence, belonging, usefulness, potency, and optimism) inventory was created and schools were asked to brainstorm practices that could build these traits, beginning with what schools already had in place (Sagor, 1996). Among the most cited activities were logical consequences for behavior, mastery expectations, service learning, cooperative learning, teacher advisory groups, authentic assessment, student-led conferences, portfolio assessment, activities programs and instruction based upon individual learning style inventories (Sagor, 1996).

Jackson (2016) set out to measure educators' effectiveness and found that grit, perseverance, and resiliency were largely to credit. Seeking to look beyond the standardized test scores that are the sole measurement of so many educator efficacy studies, Jackson became intrigued with the larger impact that some teachers had on their students—being able to convey deep messages about belonging, connection, ability and opportunity (Jackson, 2016). These messages translated into the students' psychology and their behavior (Tough, 2016).

Rather than relying on the ubiquitous standardized test scores and the four traditional pieces of data for measurement (attendance, suspensions, on-time grade progression, and overall GPA), Jackson (2016) created a proxy measure of noncognitive ability. As a rough measure of student engagement, the index turned out to be a better predictor than students' test scores of important outcomes such as college attendance, adult wages, and future arrests (Jackson, 2016). The conversation then turned to understand how teachers were effective in creating this engagement.

The classroom environment created by these teachers, imbued with messages of positivity, encouraged students to make good choices, show up to school, try harder, work longer at difficult tasks, and deal more resiliently with the slings and arrows of typical school days and beyond (Tough, 2016). The remaining question sought to identify if these were skills or, rather, a specific way of thinking about the world and attitudes that were intricately connected to behavioral choices.

Farrington et al. (2012) questioned which messages were most efficacious in building student resiliency and how these messages were conveyed from teacher to student. Farrington et al. (2012) doubted that working directly with students on changing their grit or resilience would effectively affect their academic persistence or self-discipline for the better, yet there was the belief that all students were more likely to persevere in schools and classrooms that helped them develop "positive mindsets and effective learning strategies" (Farrington et al., 2012, p. 7) Academic perseverance, Farrington and her colleagues found, was the phenomenon of maintaining positive academic behaviors despite failure or, more specifically, a resilient attitude toward failure (Farrington et al., 2012).

Students with this persistence did not give up or become angry or frustrated; instead, they looked for new ways to master material or solve problem; however, Farrington et al. (2012) discovered that perseverance and academic resiliency were highly contextually dependent, not necessarily stable over time. Teachers were found to have a profound impact on developing this resiliency by allowing students to build a sense of competence through achievement by lessening the chances of student frustration boiling over, and/or reducing a student's tendency to give up and withdraw (Farrington et al., 2012).

Farrington et al. (2012) drilled down into the research further and extracted four key beliefs that students need to persevere to include "(1) I belong in this academic community, (2) My ability and competence grow with my effort, (3) I can succeed at this, and (4) This work has value for me" (p. 9). Tough (2016) remarked on the disparity between how those who had had typical childhoods and those who had suffered toxic-stress exposure react to these beliefs. In challenging situations, those who suffered Adverse Childhood Experiences (ACEs) are apt to react with opposite warnings, the fight or flight syndrome—as in, "I don't belong here. . . . Everyone in this school is out to get me" (Tough, 2016, n.p.).

The fact that these students are more prone to being academically behind their peers fuels this response, making it likely that they will act out in ways that will have behavioral, as well as academic, consequences (Tough, 2016). They are more likely to be retained, placed in special education classes or remedial classes, or suffer disciplinary consequences that predispose them to reject the key beliefs espoused by Farrington et al. (2012).

Chapter 6

PROGRAMS TO CREATE KINDER SCHOOLS AND CYBERSPACE

Schools have the power within them to make strides in creating more peaceable places for students to learn and grow according to Klein (2012).

> Particularly successful programs build close-knit communities where students and faculty feel valued and appreciated—and where some of the damaging socialization . . . can be transformed. Indeed, small schools are often heralded as the answer to school violence, but they are not particularly effective without focused efforts on changing the community culture (p. 205).

Some schools, such as the consortium of thirty-nine New York State schools that have opted out of high-stakes testing, see the debilitating effects of endless assessment and ranking (Klein, 2012). Believing that this leads to hierarchical and judgmental comparisons between and among students, the consortium has instead opted for more individualized forms of assessing students' learning and challenge students to create portfolios and other demonstrations based on their passions and future plans (Klein, 2012). In these schools, students are both challenged and supported and come to view diversity in learning and interests as a healthy thing.

When students and adults work together in schools on academic and community projects, there is a greater likelihood of social bonds being formed as they "appreciate themselves and each other and . . . develop the meaningful relationships that all people crave" (Klein, 2012, p. 6). Peaceful interactions and academic excellence and creativity are more prevalent in schools that have transformed their cultures in these manners.

This inclusive approach has been embedded in mentoring and community service projects, as well as leadership training (Klein, 2012). The expectation was that as individuals with visible, powerful positions, it was incumbent upon these student-athletes to exert the kind of leadership that embraced all members of the school community and stepped in to demonstrate their leadership when any member was being bullied, isolated, marginalized, or discriminated against (Klein, 2012).

One program curriculum relies on using mentors from local high schools and colleges to teach an intensive curriculum to middle school girls about being sensitive to diversity, developing emotional intelligences, appreciating their strengths, and standing up to injustices against the LGBQT+ community (Klein, 2012).

There are also "collective courage" programs around the country that

> encourage people to support one another so much and so often that students can start to feel assured that if they reach out to someone they are bound to get help

from other people in the vicinity who will also stand up for their values (Klein, 2012, p. 210).

The concept behind these programs is to raise awareness about the power of language, encourage students to act together in courageous and leader-like ways, and stand up when they witness incidents of cruelty. Such initiatives address the pressures on boys and girls to behave and to judge others on narrowly prescribed definitions of what it means to be a man or woman and instead work to break down barriers to understanding others through peer mediation training for both boys and girls (Klein, 2012).

Challenge Days are another powerful activity that evolved from Mahatma Gandhi's famous phrase, "Be the Change" (Challenge Day, 2018). Prior to the daylong training, schools put together "change teams" consisting of students and teachers who plan activities, community service, and mentoring programs designed to create a more positive school culture. The trick in making this program successful, organizers found, is that all members of a school community must have an opportunity to take part and be part, ensuring that all factions are represented and having their voices and ideas heard. (Challenge Day, 2018). Successful initiatives also are derived from individual schools that create their own models to fit identified needs.

Any such interventions depend on students and staff learning what Rosenberg (2003) described as nonviolent or compassionate communication. There are four major components of this communication style that is intended to teach how to communicate constructively with others in a face-to-face format (Rosenberg, 2003). It moves individuals away from passive-aggressive (talking or gossiping behind someone's back), passive (addressing only the other person's needs) or aggressive (bullying) to a communication style that allows students to state their own needs respectfully while still honoring another's (Rosenberg, 2003).

To do so, students need to learn how to differentiate observation from evaluation or judgment, differentiate feelings and emotions and to be able to express feelings without blame/criticism/judgment, to connect with others' and one's own human needs, and to be able to request what one would like or do not want in ways that are genuine and not demanding, guilt-evoking or shaming (Rosenberg, 2003).

THE ROLE OF SCHOOL CLIMATE AND CULTURE

Shapiro & Purpel (2004) authored an influential book on the importance of a school's culture and climate and noted that so many problems in education arose from seemingly inevitable cultural problems. When negative school cultures exist, Shapiro and Purpel (2004) said, school leaders, staff and teachers must devote inordinate amounts of their time dealing with behavioral infractions, decreasing the time and energy they have for creating a nurturing and safe school environment. The authors argued for educational leaders being more intentional in their efforts to create caring, thoughtful, and humane schools, as those students are then better supported and can function with optimal independence. This independence is fostered when students have self-management skills in the academic, social, and emotional spheres (Shapiro & Purpel, 2004).

When students are responsible members of the school community they can act independently, have some autonomy, and make decisions regarding their own behavior (Crawford & Hagedorn, 2009). This helps to build a school culture in which the behavioral expectations within the student body socially mirror the behavioral expectations that are set by the school disciplinary system (Crawford & Hagedorn, 2009). The way students act in terms of their behavior benefits their individual academic and social goals and it also can benefit fellow students and the community (Crawford & Hagedorn, 2009).

The time that school administrators and staff spend investing in teaching students the social and emotional skills of self-management is very important (Crawford & Hagedorn, 2009). The results of this time investment will include a healthy and functional school climate, the best possible setting for academic excellence, supportive classrooms, and the most ethical and moral school structure (Crawford &Hagedorn, 2009; O'Connor et al., 2011).

Behavioral systems cannot operate independent of the cultural values of a school; those values should aim toward the creation of responsible and independent learners (Crawford &Hagedorn, 2009). When a school's behavioral system is founded upon expectations that are socially responsible and align positively with that school's culture, students begin to automatically connect prosocial behavior with acts that demonstrate that they care deeply for others in their school and see themselves as an important cog in their learning and social environments (Crawford & Hagedorn, 2009). Such learners look out for one another, are more inclusive and comfortable with differences, and are less likely to need to act out to try to earn respect, attention or membership (O'Connor et al., 2011).

In a large study on the role of school climate in school violence, Hurford et al. (2010) found that perceived school climate was intertwined with cultures of bullying and other forms of violence. When students perceived favored groups such as "the preps" or "the jocks" had higher status and received preferential treatment, there were more prevalent feelings of not being safe, of bullying, and reports of being threatened with weapons at school (Hurford et al., 2010).

Schools in which there were strict hierarchies and where there was little tolerance for individual differences were more likely to have a bully culture, and this was also true when adults modeled clear preferences for particular groups and meted out discipline more harshly to others; adult bullying also increased the chances for a bully culture among students (Hurford et al., 2010). The authors found that classroom climate and school ecology mattered greatly. Schools with a warm environment, clear and consistent codes of conduct, and leadership that modeled respect for all students and receptivity to ideas from diverse student constituencies had less violent behavior (Hurford et al., 2010).

Those schools that offered bullying training to all students and avoided favoritism had healthier climates as did schools in which students believed that if they went to teachers and administration when they were fearful, had witnessed bullying, or had been made aware of the presence of a weapon in school, there would be appropriate follow-up by the adults in charge (Hurford et al., 2010). When victims of bullying or other forms of violence received adequate social support that buffered the outcomes of stress, they were less likely subsequently to want to retaliate against others and more likely to function with better mental and emotional health (Hurford et al., 2010).

This study emphasizes the crucial role that adults in the school building, especially those in leadership roles, have in setting a tone for inclusion, respect, valuing difference, and meting out any necessary discipline according to clear and consistent guidelines (Hurford et al., 2010). When adults deal with students or other adults in disparaging ways, or with inequitable treatment, they lay the foundation for a culture of violence or social isolation. In addition to their leadership stance, they can also bring valuable clubs, organizations, and speakers into their schools to promote a prosocial environment that diminishes the alienation and marginalization that can lead some students to violent actions.

CLUBS AND ORGANIZATIONS

SAVE Promise clubs exist around the United States and Canada (National SAVE, 2017). Founded after a seventeen-year-old student athlete in West Charlotte, North Carolina attempted to break up a challenge by a rival gang who showed up to interfere with a party (National SAVE, 2017). Alex Orange was shot and killed in this attempt and it propelled his classmates to turn their mourning into Students Against Violence Everywhere (SAVE).

The organization, which is student-led and can be a stand-alone club or merge with others such as Students Against Drunk Driving or Student Council, aims to educate and empower students to become powerful forces against violence within their schools before it happens (National SAVE, 2017). In 2017, the national group merged with Sandy Hook Promise to promote an even wider campaign against all forms of violence and victimization (National SAVE, 2017).

These initiatives have a three-part approach to developing kinder and safer schools (National SAVE, 2017).

- Start with Hello: stresses social skills and outreach to all students within the community and reduces the chances that there are marginalized students or groups and recognizes that all students must make efforts to reach out to others, especially those who may be on the fringes of mainstream school culture (National SAVE, 2017).
- Say Something: teaches students to speak to trusted adults and resources if they see behaviors or hear things that concern them or seem out of the ordinary. This stance stresses that all school community members are responsible both to act, rather than be bystanders, and report on what they hear that may give indications of individual or group problems, actions or attitudes that are not consistent with school-wide tolerance and acceptance.
- Signs of Suicide (SOS): is a deliberate training in the symptoms and signs of depression and suicidal ideation or planning to prevent students from moving from disengagement to actual attempts.

RACHEL'S CHALLENGE AND AWAKEN THE LEARNER

As discussed earlier, Rachel Scott was the first student shot and killed at Columbine High School. In her memory, her family established Rachel's Challenge, a national program featuring speakers (some of whom survived the massacre) to assist schools in setting up chapters of the challenge (Rachel's Challenge, n.d.a). Beyond these powerful presentations, each middle or high school engages in either an Awaken, Sustain, or Immerse program, followed by the Chain Reaction training that includes

> high-energy activities, interaction with caring adults, and engagement in relevant discussion regarding bullying, painful life experiences, and emotional expression, Chain Reaction is designed to draw students together, break down barriers, and influence students to make changes. Students respond to the day's challenges with self-reflection and the acknowledgment of personal responsibility. The day concludes with a final exercise called Cross the Line, where students are challenged to openly admit their life struggles and failures—breaking down barriers and encouraging honest self-disclosure among peers. (Rachel's Challenge, n.d.b)

The program can be administered grade by grade, level by level, or across different (and inclusive of all) groups and cliques within a school. One goal is to reach out to marginalized groups and "leaders at promise" (not necessarily the most visible school leaders) to build a larger cadre of those who can then work with their peers (Rachel's Challenge, n.d.b).

For younger audiences, there are elementary programs in which they discuss using kind words, refraining from bullying, prejudice, and isolation, and "how one person can make a difference" (Rachel's Challenge, n.d.c). This program also follows the Awaken, Sustain, and Immerse program objectives that are part of the Awaken the Learner framework (Rachel's Challenge, n.d.c).

Awaken the Learner is a collaboration between Rachel Scott's father and well-known author and educational researcher Richard Marzano who worked together to develop programs that "awaken the learner" in all domains (Scott & Marzano, 2014). As Scott read the final journal entry of his slain daughter, Rachel, he read of her desire for a life of meaning and purpose—the passionate purpose in life that he was inspired to help all learners discover (Scott & Marzano, 2014). Scott differentiated the why of education (purpose) from the how (process) and what (performance or end result) and realized that too heavy an emphasis was being placed on the latter two in contemporary American education (Scott & Marzano, 2014). Awaken the heart first, he argued, and the rest will follow (Scott & Marzano, 2014).

Traditional philosophies of awakening always stressed the importance of touching the heart before imparting cognitive knowledge (head) and translating that knowledge into action (hands) (Scott & Marzano, 2014). In workshops on awakening the learning, the emphasis is on how teachers can first reach the heart of all students so that they are motivated to persevere through the hard work of becoming competent at their passion and learning goal-setting, self-regulation, problem-solving skills and self-assessment necessary to become a lifelong learner (Scott & Marzano, 2014).

The program is based on other beliefs, as well, including adopting a "be the change" attitude, focusing on solving problems rather than the problems themselves, and seeing beyond surface appearances of individuals to a deeper, more soulful view (Scott & Marzano, 2014). The authors believe that too many educators adhere to the notion of students as the soil in which teachers will plant the seeds of knowledge; yet, they argue that educators should believe

> ... that students already have everything built into them for growth and maturity, the teacher provides the right climate and culture for the seeds to flourish. The facts, figures, and information are simply nutrients that the healthy seed can absorb to aid in its growth. Consider this: a watermelon seed does not have to

be taught how to produce a watermelon. Everything that seed needs to become a watermelon is already locked inside (p. 58).

The classroom environment, however, needs to be nurturing, and some students will have tougher "seed coats" than others; thus, they require more coaxing to sprout. The elements of that environment include security, so that students do not have to try to learn and grow while their adrenal systems are pumped up with fear or distrust; a sense of unique identity; and belonging (Scott & Marzano, 2014).

The skillful teacher integrates three kinds of nurturing into his or her classroom to include setting high expectations for all learners; providing encouragement; and displaying expressions (since 70 percent of communication in a classroom is nonverbal) that tells each student s/he is valued, respected, and can succeed (Scott & Marzano, 2014). Teachers are urged, therefore, to consider different physical layouts for the classroom, the "scenery" to create a positive atmosphere, and the "senses" being involved in all learning (Scott & Marzano, 2014).

The awakening classroom has a positive emotional environment. Special attention is paid to developing positive peer relationships so that no one is marginalized, and all learners contribute (Scott & Marzano, 2014). Teachers rely a great deal on materials, literature, and history of individuals who have set positive examples, overcome challenges, and made powerful impacts on the world, and believe in the use of such a curriculum to inspire their students and utilize personal projects that tap individual interests and desires to make a difference (Scott & Marzano, 2014). Mindfulness is taught and used and students learn how to cultivate self-efficacy through individual strategies to face and persist through academic challenges (Scott & Marzano, 2014).

Scott & Marzano (2014) believe in a curriculum that openly acknowledges and discusses individual differences, while also helps students see similarities among all people and cultures. Other noteworthy attributes of this curriculum include

- An emphasis is on relatedness and celebrating unity with an intentional curriculum focus that helps students learn to be peacemakers.
- Rather than focusing on problems such as bullying, students learn to separate the bully from the behavior, practicing positive regard for the person while not ignoring the behavior.
- Students are taught that ignoring a negative behavior increases its persistence, so they must reach for the heart of the bully and affirm him or her as an individual while stating opposition to the bullying actions.
- Students learn to reinforce all small acts of prosocial behavior and also recognize their own responsibility to model the behavior that they wish to observe in others. (Scott & Marzano, 2014)

THE NECESSITY OF PARENTAL AND COMMUNITY INVOLVEMENT

Strategies, interventions, and organizations only work when families and communities are actively involved in the process. Ferlazzo (2013) has long argued that there is a vast difference between "involved" parents and "engaged" parents, with engaged parents becoming the articulators of what families need and taking leadership roles in suggesting and implementing programs that matter.

Ferlazzo and Hammond (2009) found that parental engagement is critical to student achievement as students with engaged parents were found to earn higher GPAs and standardized test scores, took risks to enroll in more challenging academic coursework, attended school more regularly, passed courses at higher rates, earned more credits, displayed improved home and school behavior, and demonstrated better social skills and adaptation to school. True family engagement also results in more positive parent/teacher relationships, more collaboration, volunteering for larger decision-making roles, as well as better student health and well-being (Ferlazzo & Hammond, 2009).

Ferlazzo and Hammond (2009) define parental engagement by making it clear that parents are viewed as potential leaders without whom school and community initiatives will not be successful. School and community staff act as organizers or coaches and also organize and deliver leadership development along the way. Very often, a family's greatest concerns and needs are less related to school and more centered on immediate needs at home and in their community (Ferlazzo & Hammond, 2009). Health, housing, economics, or safety concerns, for example, are often salient in parents' lives. Savvy educators know that all of those variables play critical roles in how well children perform in school and what energy and time families have to invest in school engagement.

In schools that engage all stakeholders in school-related functions, parents and community members are polled for their own needs, priorities, and ideas for change (Ferlazzo & Hammond, 2009). Parental and community energy motivate these relationships as these individuals feel more and more challenged to do something about these needs and priorities; in turn, school personnel feel comfortable giving up some of the reins of control and trust their constituents to act on children's behalf.

In the arena of school safety and well-being, family members need both information and the skills and attitudes to transmit the importance of this information to their children. This entails inviting them into conversations about their concerns and their suggestions for improving school and community safety and well-being (Cowan & Paine, 2013). The national organization for school psychologists stresses the critical role of nurturing environments, at home and in the community, to augment the work of schools. Safety and learning, the document's authors write, go hand in hand (Cowan & Paine, 2013). Schools must work with family and community members to identify the ways in which they can minimize children's exposure to toxic events and environments while reinforcing prosocial behaviors and fostering resiliency.

According to Ferlazzo and Hammond (2009) engagement must be expressed in three distinct ways to include the previously mentioned mandate that schools use all means that they can to determine families' true needs, goals, aspirations, and concerns. Schools must expand their role to include developing "social capital," which can be defined as the value that an individual can gain from having social connections, networks, and an understanding of how to navigate social institutions (Ferlazzo & Hammond, 2009).

Schools should look to maximize opportunities in which families can use previous knowledge such as what they know and have experienced, and the skills, attitudes, and problem-solving approaches they have garnered from these experiences, to enrich the school (Ferlazzo & Hammond, 2009). Families and community members, especially in marginalized groups, have a wealth of experience in overcoming challenges and can be valuable contributors to school safety and wellness endeavors if their knowledge is put to good use (Ferlazzo & Hammond, 2009).

A school or community cannot truly be safe unless both physical and psychological safety exist for all members (Cowan & Paine, 2013). Schools also cannot become fortresses, as in many communities, especially those that are low-income, rural, or small, the school itself is the community center. The school-community partnership is a coordinated dance in which the daily safety and mental health programming are guided by relevant school personnel, while the community supplies resources such as social services and mental health agencies, first responders, mentors, and youth programs and facilities.

Rollison et al. (2013) articulate the need for better interagency collaboration in the delivery of services to students, noting that this can minimize duplication of services, make best use of scarce resources, and serve at-risk or those children and adolescents already touched by violence of any kind.

STUDENT ENGAGEMENT

A final piece of the school safety picture involves student engagement. After being involved in or vicariously affected by so many school shootings and other acts of violence, some students have become shell-shocked, numb, or resolved to the presence of violence in our society; yet others have become resistant to those disengaged emotions (Jonsson, 2018). Students like Carson

Collins of Aztec High School, who experienced a school shooting in December of 2017, have vowed not to develop a siege mentality explaining, "When you think about it, it's like you get punched in the gut . . . and then they tell you to smile. I'm not prepared to smile" (Jonsson, 2018, p. 1). Instead of smiling, Collins became politically active, turning fear and anger into what he hopes will be societal change (Jonsson, 2018).

One change in student activism, which dates back to the Columbine aftermath, is that contemporary students seem more willing to engage in dialogue, even with those whose views they do not support (Jonsson, 2018). Recognizing the polarizing issue of gun control, students are looking to voter registration, as well as events such as marches, to effect change. Yet, they recognize the importance in remembering both the victims of gun violence and "the people on the other side of the aisle, we're also doing this for them," remarked Nathan Dominquez, a student activist. "We can't make them out as our enemy. Those are our fellow Americans and they're important in this process" (Aouslin & Ingram, 2018, n.p.).

Turning fear, anger, and grief into positive actions is one way to help students ward off depression, debilitating rage, and withdrawal. Part of school well-being is becoming involved, not only in one's studies and the school community, but in larger social issues that matter to students, so that there are outlets to channel emotions that might otherwise become purely negative and interfere with overall health and future optimism.

FINAL THOUGHTS

Contemporary schools are extremely complex and multifaceted institutions that face the daunting task of educating children and adolescents in a rapidly diversifying society. This entails creating warm, safe, orderly, and welcoming environments that allow youth to reach their potential and become productive, creative, contributing citizens as adults. In order to fulfill this lofty mission, schools must integrate services and marshal all of their resources (academic, social, emotional, environmental, and mental health and well-being) in a coordinated fashion. By using these resources effectively, schools can lessen behavioral and mental health problems that can escalate into violence or self-harm, and improve the communications, interactions, and well-being of all school members.

The hallmarks of schools that build a peaceable kingdom share many common traits. Among them are student engagement, a dedicated health and wellness curriculum, positive discipline, school connectedness and relational education, parent-school-community partnerships, alternative discipline protocols, and well-articulated and enforced policies to address such issues as bullying, harassment, and microaggressions (APA, 2018b). Schools view it as their role to educate in a whole child fashion and work to build resilience and academic perseverance that will increase the likelihood of student success and self-esteem, while diminishing behavioral problems and disengagement.

Peaceful schools also forge strong partnerships with others, bolstering the resources that exist within the school building and spreading awareness to other key constituents such as family and community members. In developing effective school safety and well-being programs, families must be truly engaged and viewed as the source of ideas and the collaborative leaders of any successful initiatives. So, too, must students, as vicarious trauma from witnessing or experiencing school violence second-hand can impact health and well-being negatively; turning righteous anger into action gives students an avenue to effecting change in a positive way. Schools so often are the pulsing heart of communities in which they are located; thus, there is incentive to ensure that they are safe and hospitable places for all individuals.

POINTS TO REMEMBER

- *School culture plays a powerful role in preventing school violence and disengagement.*
- *Feeling a sense of belonging, being valued, treated equitably, and recognized for one's unique talents and contributions are necessary components of feeling safe, connected to, and engaged in one's school community.*
- *Healthy schools have intentional curriculum and programming around issues of mental health, teen suicide, bullying, and other forms of aggressive behavior, including relational aggression.*
- *Students and staff need clear, uniformly enforced discipline codes and must be aware of available resources within their school community if they observe or hear of troubling behavior or thoughts, such as suicidal ideation.*
- *There is a growing body of research that supports the use of alternative forms of discipline and such practices as yoga, meditation, and mindfulness to lower stress, boost self-regulation, and reduce aggressive behaviors.*
- *Positive and alternative forms of discipline may help to reduce violent behavior and create cohesion in the school community, as behavioral norms for all school community members are similar and addressed with consistency.*
- *Infusing the curriculum with the social and emotional aspects of learning, as well as teaching nonviolent communication, can give students tools with which to interact more hospitably with one another while still getting important needs met.*

- *All successful initiatives to prevent school violence rely on education and engagement of parents, students, and community members.*
- *Student engagement in the school safety issue is equally important so that their voices are heard, and they do not become emotional casualties of acts of violence.*
- *Schools and community agencies need better coordination of services in order to use scarce resources efficiently, minimize duplication of services, and reach all youth at-risk or who have been touched by violence or neglect.*

References

Abbasi, M.A., Saeidi, M., Khademi, G., Hoseini, B.L., & Moghadam, Z.E. (2015). Child maltreatment in the worldwide: A review article. *International Journal of Pediatrics, 3*(1–1), 353–365. Retrieved from www.http://ijp.mums.ac.ir

Acosta, J., Chinman, M., Ebener, P., Malone, P.S., Phillips, A., & Wilks, A. (2018). Understanding the relationship between perceived school climate and bullying: A mediator analysis. *Journal of School Violence.* DOI: 10.1080/15388220.2018.1453820

Adelman, H.S., & Taylor, L. (2010). *Mental health in schools: Engaging learners, preventing problems, and improving schools.* Thousand Oaks, CA: Corwin.

Afzaal, A. (2012). *The violence triangle.* Retrieved from https://ahmedafzaal.com/2012/02/20/the-violence-triangle/

Ahmed, S., & Walker, C. (2018). School shootings so far in 2018. Retrieved from https://www.cnn.com/2018/03/02/us/school-shootings-2018-list-trnd/index.html

Allen, S. (2018). Here's what happened when a school replaced detention with meditation. Retrieved from https://www.doyouyoga.com/heres-what-happened-when-a-school-replaced-detention-with-meditation-54737/

AiRISTA Flow. (2016). *Secure schools: Six key areas for violence prevention and safety enhancement.* Retrieved from https://www.airistaflow.com/wp-content/uploads/2016/07/AiRISTA-Flow-School-Safety.pdf

American Academy of Pediatrics [AAP]. (2014). Adverse childhood experiences and the lifelong consequences of trauma. Retrieved from https://www.aap.org/en-us/Documents/ttb_aces_consequences.pdf

American Academy of Pediatrics [AAP]. (2018). *Promoting resilience.* Retrieved from https://www.aap.org/en-us/advocacy-and-policy/aap-health-initiatives/resilience/Pages/Promoting-Resilience.aspx

American Association of University Women [AAUW]. (1992). *How schools shortchange girls: The AAUW report: A study of major findings on girls and education.* Retrieved from https://history.aauw.org/aauw-research/1992-how-schools-shortchange-girls

American Foundation for Suicide Prevention [AFSP]. (2018). *Risk factors and warning signs.* Retrieved from https://afsp.org/about-suicide/risk-factors-and-warning-signs/

American Institute of Stress [AIS]. (2018). *Compassion fatigue.* Retrieved from https://www.stress.org/military/for-practitionersleaders/compassion-fatigue/

American Psychological Association [APA]. (2018a). *Bullying and school climate.* Retrieved from http://www.apa.org/advocacy/interpersonal-violence/bullying-school-climate.aspx

American Psychological Association [APA]. (2018b). *School connectedness.* Retrieved from http://www.apa.org/pi/lgbt/programs/safe-supportive/school-connectedness/default.aspx

Anderson, M. (2016). *Here's how schools can support students' mental health.* Retrieved from https://www.npr.org/sections/ed/2016/09/20/459843929/heres-how-schools-can-support-students-mental-health

Anderson, M., & Cardoza, K. (2016). *Mental health in schools: A hidden crisis affecting millions of students.* Retrieved from https://www.npr.org/sections/ed/2016/08/31/464727159/mental-health-in-schools-a-hidden-crisis-affecting-millions-of-students

Asoulin, R., & Ingram, N. (2018). *After mass shootings, students hope to change sense of siege to surge in activism.* Retrieved from https://www.msn.com/en-gb/news/us/after-mass-shootings-students-hope-to-change-sense-of-siege-to-surge-in-activism/ar-AAxFfLk?li=BBnbcA1

Associated Press. (2018). *A history of school shootings in the United States.* Retrieved from http://www.sun-sentinel.com/local/broward/parkland/florida-school-shooting/fl-reg-school-shooting-list-20180214-story.html

Banks, A., & Hirschman, L.A. (2016). *Wired to connect: The surprising link between brain science and strong, healthy relationships.* New York, NY: Penguin/Random House.

Barrett, S., Eber, L., & Weist, M. (n.d.). *Advancing education effectiveness: Interconnecting school mental health and school-wide positive behavior.* Retrieved from https://www.pbis.org/common/cms/files/Current%20Topics/Final-Monograph.pdf

Bates, L. (2017). *Are we ignoring an epidemic of sexual violence in schools?* Retrieved from https://www.theguardian.com/lifeandstyle/2017/dec/12/are-we-ignoring-an-epidemic-of-sexual-violence-in-schools

Bauer, G.F. (2017). The application of salutogenesis in everyday settings. In M. Mittlemark et al. (Eds.), *The handbook of salutogenesis,* 153–158. DOI: 10.1007?978-3-319-04600-6_16

Beegle, D. (2009). *Education students from generational poverty: Building blocks from a to z.* Retrieved from http://www.mrleasure.com/uploads/6/4/0/6/6406507/educating-students-poverty.pdf

Bekiempis, V. (2014). Nearly 1 in 5 Americans suffer from mental health each year. *Newsweek.* Retrieved from http://www.newsweek.com/nearly-1-5-americans-suffer-mental-illness-each-year-230608

Benbenishty, R., Astor, R.A., Roziner, I., & Wrabel, S.L. (2016). Testing the causal links between school climate, school violence, and school academic performance:

References

A cross-lagged panel autoregressive model. *Education Researcher, 45*(3), 197–206. DOI: 10.3102/0013189X16644603

Benevento, M. (2018). *City Connects program addresses all factors that affect student success.* Retrieved from https://www.ncronline.org/news/people/city-connects-program-addresses-all-factors-affect-student-success

Berger, T. (2018). *An inside look at trauma-informed practices.* Retrieved from https://www.edutopia.org/article/inside-look-trauma-informed-practices

Bertrand, M., & Pan, J. (2011). *The trouble with the boys: Social influences and the gender gap in disruptive behavior.* Retrieved from: http://www.nber.org/papers/w17541.pdf

Bloom, D. (2016). *Instead of detention, these students get meditation.* Retrieved from https://www.cnn.com/2016/11/04/health/meditation-in-schools-baltimore/index.html

Blueprints for Healthy Youth Development. (2018). *Programs.* Retrieved from https://www.blueprintsprograms.org/

Borum, R. (2015). Targeted violence in schools. In P.M. Kleespies (Ed.), *The Oxford handbook of behavioral emergencies and crises.* DOI: 10.1093/oxfordhb/9780199352722.013.9

Bosworth, K., & Judkins, M. (2014). Tapping into the power of school climate to prevent bullying: One application of schoolwide positive behavior interventions and supports. *Theory into Practice, 53*(4), 300–307.

Breiding, M.J., Basile, K.C., Smith, M.C., & Mahendra, R. (2015). *Intimate partner violence surveillance: Uniform definitions and recommended data elements.* Retrieved from https://www.cdc.gov/violenceprevention/pdf/intimatepartnerviolence.pdf

Bridging Refugee Youth & Children's Services [BRYCS]. (n.d.) *Refugee children in US schools: A toolkit for teachers and personnel.* Retrieved from http://www.brycs.org/documents/upload/bullying.pdf

Buchmann, C., DiPrete T., & McDaniel, A. (2008). Gender inequalities in education. *Annual Review of Sociology, 34*, 319–337. DOI: 10.1146/annurev.soc.34.040507.134719

Butchart, A., Mikton, C., Dahlberg, L.L., & Krug, E.G. (2014). Global status report on violence prevention 2014. *Injury Prevention, 21*(3), 213. DOI: 10.1136/injuryprev-2015-041640

Calderon, V.J., & Yu, D. (2017). *Student enthusiasm falls as high school graduation nears.* Retrieved from http://news.gallup.com/opinion/gallup/211631/student-enthusiasm-falls-high-school-graduation-nears.aspx

Capp, G., Moore, H., Pitner, R., Iachini, A., Berkowitz, R., Astor, R.A., & Benbenishty, R. (2017). School violence. *Oxford Research Encyclopedia of Education.* DOI: 10.1093/acrefore/9780190264093.013.78

CASEL. (2018). *What is SEL?* Retrieved from https://casel.org/what-is-sel/

Celli, L.M., & Young, N.D. (2014). *Learning style perspectives: Impact in the classroom* (3rd ed.). Madison, WI: Atwood Publishers.

Centers for Disease Control and Prevention. (2016). *Understanding school violence: Fact sheet.* Retrieved from https://www.cdc.gov/violenceprevention/pdf/School_Violence_Fact_Sheet-a.pdf

Centers for Disease Control and Prevention. (2017). *School violence: Prevention tools and resources.* Retrieved from https://www.cdc.gov/violenceprevention/youthviolence/schoolviolence/tools.html

Chaisson, K.E. (2013). *Examining the relations among trauma, distress, resilience, and physical health.* Retrieved from http://scholarworks.uark.edu/cgi/viewcontent.cgi?article=1930&context=etd

Challenge Days. (2018). *Be the change team guide.* Retrieved from https://www.challengeday.org/be-the-change-team-guide/

City of Minneapolis. (2012). *Minneapolis blueprint for action to prevent youth violence.* Retrieved from http://www.minneapolismn.gov/www/groups/public/@health/documents/webcontent/wcms1p-114466.pdf

Cohen, J.A. (2015). New research in treating child and adolescent trauma. *PRSD Research Quarterly, 26*(3), 1–3. Retrieved from https://www.ptsd.va.gov/professional/newsletters/research-quarterly/V26N3.pdf

Cohn, R.D., & Mohl, R.A. (1979). *The paradox of progressive education: The Gary Plan and urban schooling.* Port Washington, NY: Kennikat Press.

Cowan, K., & Paine, C. (2013). School safety: What really works. *Principal Leadership, 13*(7), 12–16. Retrieved from http://connection.ebscohost.com/c/articles/85948249/school-safety-what-really-works

Cowan, K.C., Vaillancourt, K., Rossen, E., & Pollitt, K. (2013). *A framework for safe and successful schools.* Retrieved from https://www.naesp.org/sites/default/files/Framework%20for%20Safe%20and%20Successful%20School%20Environments_FINAL_0.pdf

Crary, D. (2014). *New survey details vast scope of teen dating abuse.* Retrieved from https://apnews.com/55da725fbf8f43bc86bb17bf3a9c7b47/new-survey-details-vast-scope-teen-dating-abuse

Crawford, L., & Hagedorn, C. (2009). *Classroom discipline: Guiding adolescents to responsible independence.* Minneapolis, MN: Origins Developmental Designs.

Crews, G.A., & Counts, M.R. (1997). *The evolution of school disturbance in America.* Westport, CT: Praeger Publishers.

Cubberly, E.P. (1934). *Public education in the United States.* New York, NY: Houghton Mifflin.

Cubberly, E.P. (1962). *Public education in the United States: A study and interpretation of American educational history.* Cambridge, MA: The Riverside Press.

Cullen, D. (2009). *Columbine.* New York, NY: Hatchette Book Group.

Davis, A. (2016). *Minnesota teachers curbing distractions with mindful meditation.* Retrieved from https://minnesota.cbslocal.com/2016/09/12/minnesota-teachers-curbing-distractions-mindful-meditation/

De Bellis, M.D., & Zisk, A. (2014). The biological effects of childhood trauma. *Child and Adolescent Psychiatric Clinics of North America, 23*(2), 185–222. DOI: 10.1016/j.chc.2014.01.002

Del Giudice, V. (2018). *U.S. mass shootings from 1949 to 2018: Summary of Incidents.* Retrieved from https://www.bloomberg.com/news/articles/2018-06-28/u-s-mass-shootings-from-1949-to-2018-summary-of-incidents

Denmark, F., Krauss, H.H., Wesner, R.W., Midlarsky, E., & Gielen, U.P. (Eds.) (2005). *Violence in schools: Cross-national and cross-cultural perspectives.* DOI: 10.1007/0-387-28811-2

Douglass, A.A. (1940). *The American school system: A survey of the principles and practices of education.* New York, NY: Farrar and Rinehart.

Duckett, P., Kagan, C., & Sixsmith, J. (2010). Consultation and participation with children in health schools. *American Journal of Community Psychology, 46*(1–2), 167–178. DOI: 10.1007/s10464-010-9327-8

Dumitriu, C. (2013). School violence around the world: A social phenomenon. *Procedia Social and Behavioral Sciences. 92*(2013), 299–308. DOI: 10.1016/j.sbspro.2013.08.676

Durlak, J.A., Weissberg, R.P., Dymnicki, A.B., Taylor, R.D., & Schellinger, K.B. (2011). The impact of enhancing students' social and emotional learning: A meta-analysis of schools-based universal interventions. *Child Development, 82*, 405–432. Retrieved from https://casel.org/the-impact-of-enhancing-students-social-and-emotional-learning-a-meta-analysis-of-school-based-universal-interventions/

Ebert, M., & Flynn, E. (2014). *An antidote to teacher burnout: How yoga and mindfulness can support resilience in and out of the classroom.* Retrieved from http://www.yoga4classrooms.com/yoga-4-classrooms-blog/Teacher-Burnout-yoga-mindfulness-for-teacher-resilience-classroom

Espelage, D., Anderman, E.M., Brown, V.E., Jones, A., Lane, K.L., McMahon, S.D., Reddy, L.A., & Reynolds, C.R. (2013). Understanding and preventing violence directed against teachers. *American Psychologist, 68*(2), 75–87. DOI: 10.1037/a0031307

Essex, N. (2012). *School law and the public schools: A practical guide for educational leaders* (5th ed.). Boston, MA: Pearson

Faeq, D. (2016). *Depression among students: Critical review.* DOI: 10.13140/RG/2.2.21978.75205

Farrington, C.A., Roderick, M., Allensworth, E., Nagaoka, J., Keyes, T.S., Johnson, D.W., & Beechum, N.O. (2012). *Teaching adolescents to become learners: The role of noncognitive factors in shaping school performance: A critical literature review.* Retrieved from https://consortium.uchicago.edu/sites/default/files/publications/Noncognitive%20Report.pdf

Ferlazzo, L. (2013). The differences between parent involvement and parent engagement. *Library Media Connection, 28.* Retrieved from https://larryferlazzo.edublogs.org/files/2013/03/LMC_March_April_2013_Ferlazzo-p3tzf9.pdf

Ferlazzo, L., & Hammond, L. (2009). *Building parental engagement in schools.* Santa Barbara, CA: Linworth.

Flannery, D.J., Wester, K.L., & Singer, M.I. (2004). Impact of exposure to violence in school on child and adolescent mental health and behavior. *Journal of Community Psychology, 32*(5), 559–573. DOI: 10.1002/jcop.20019

Ford, Z. (2014). *Over half of LGBT students feel unsafe at school, report shows.* Retrieved from https://thinkprogress.org/over-half-of-lgbt-students-feel-unsafe-at-school-report-shows-22d6fdc52b98/

Freeman, J., Kowitt, J., Simonsen, B., Wei, Y., Dooley, K., Gordon, L., & Maddock, E. (2018). A high school replication of targeted professional development for classroom management. *Remedial and Special Education, 39*(3), 144–157. DOI: 10.1177/0741932517719547

Frick, P.J. (2016). Current research on conduct disorder I children and adolescents. *South African Journal of Psychology, 46*(2), 160–174. DOI: 10.1177/0081246316628455

Friedrich, A.A., Mendez, L.M., & Mihalas, S.T. (2010). Gender as a factor in school-based mental health services delivery. *School Psychology Review, 39*(1), 122–136. Retrieved from https://www.nasponline.org/publications/periodicals/spr/volume-39/volume-39-issue-1/gender-as-a-factor-in-school-based-mental-health-service-delivery

Fronius, T., Persson, H., Guckenburg, S., Hurley, N., & Petrosino, A. (2016). Restorative justice in U.A. schools: A research review. Retrieved from https://jprc.wested.org/wp-content/uploads/2016/02/RJ_Literature-Review_20160217.pdf

Gaastra, G.F., Groen, Y., Tucha, L., & Tucha, O. (2016). The effects of classroom interventions on off-task and disruptive classroom behavior in children with symptoms of attention-deficit/hyperactivity disorder: A meta-analysis review. *PLoS One, 11*(2): e0148841. DOI: 10.1371/journal.pone.0148841

Gallop Report. (2014). *State of America's schools: The path to winning again in education.* Retrieved from https://www.gallup.com/services/178709/state-america-schools-report.aspx

Garbarino, J. (1995). Growing up in a socially toxic environment: Life for children and families in the 1990s. In G.B. Melton (Ed.), *The individual, the family, and the social good: Personal fulfillment in times of change*, 1–20. Lincoln: University of Nebraska Press.

Garmezy, N., Masten, A.S., & Tellegen, A. (1984). The study of stress and competence in children: A building block for developmental psychopathology. *Child Development, 55*(1), 97–111. DOI: 10.2307/1129837

Gellerman, B. (2014). It was like a war zone: Busing in Boston. Retrieved from http://www.wbur.org/news/2014/09/05/boston-busing-anniversary

Gibbs, B. (2015). *The importance of the relational teacher.* Retrieved from https://www.thersa.org/discover/publications-and-articles/rsa-blogs/2015/09/the-importance-of-the-relational-teacher

Gordon, C. (2014). *By the numbers: Sexual violence in high school.* Retrieved from http://america.aljazeera.com/watch/shows/america-tonight/articles/2014/11/14/by-the-numbers-sexualviolenceinhighschool.html

Gordon, E.W., & Song, L.D. (1994). Variations in the experience of resilience. In M.C. Wang & E.W. Gordon (Eds.), *Educational resilience in inner-city America: Challenges and prospects*, 27–44. Mahwah, NJ: Lawrence Erlbaum Associates.

Gray, P. (2014). *The danger of back to school.* Retrieved from https://www.psychologytoday.com/us/blog/freedom-learn/201408/the-danger-back-school

Green, A. (2016). *10 common mental health problems students face.* Retrieved from http://www.edudemic.com/student-mental-health/

Hartford, T.C., Hsiao-ye, Y., & Freeman, R.C. (2012). A typology of violence against self and others and its associations with drinking and other drug use among high school students in a U.S. general population survey. *Journal of Child and Adolescence Substance Abuse, 21*(4), 349–366. DOI: 10.1080/1067828X.2012.710028

Haupt, A. (2016). *Mindfulness in schools: When meditation replaces detention.* Retrieved from https://health.usnews.com/wellness/mind/articles/2016-12-08/mindfulness-in-schools-when-meditation-replaces-detention

Henderson, N., & Milstein, M.M. (2002). *Resiliency in schools: Making in happen for students and educators.* Thousand Oaks, CA: Corwin.

Hickey, L. (2014). *The patterns in mass shootings and a conversation about men.* Retrieved from https://goodmenproject.com/ethics-values/patterns-mass-shootings-conversation-men/

Hill, C., & Kearl, H. (2011). *Crossing the line: Sexual harassment at school.* Retrieved from http://files.eric.ed.gov/fulltext/ED525785.pdf

Hoagwood, K., Burns, B.J., Kiser, L., Ringeisen, H., & Schoenwalkd, S.K. (2001). Evidence-based practice in child and adolescent mental health services. *Psychiatric Services, 52*, 1179–1189. DOI: 10.1176/appi.ps.52.9.1179

Huang, B. (2014). *Gender bias faced by girls and what we can do.* Los Angeles, CA: The Center for Mental Health in Schools at UCLA. Retrieved from http://smhp.psych.ucla.edu/

Hurford, D.P., Lindskog, R., Cole, A., Jackson, R. Thomasson, S., & Wade, A. (2010). The role of school climate in school violence: A validity study of a web-based school violence study. *Journal of Educational Research & Policy Studies, 10*(1), 51–77. Retrieved from https://eric.ed.gov/?id=EJ930165

Jackson, C.K. (2016). *What do test scores miss? The importance of teacher effects on non-test score outcomes.* Retrieved from https://www.ipr.northwestern.edu/publications/docs/workingpapers/2016/WP-16-03.pdf

Jensen, E. (2009). *Teaching with poverty in mind: What being poor does to kids' brains and what schools can do about it.* Alexandria, VA: ASCD.

Jonsson, P. (2018). After mass shootings, students hope to change sense of siege to surge in activism. *Christian Science Monitor.* Retrieved from https://www.msn.com/en-us/news/us/after-mass-shootings-students-hope-to-change-sense-of-siege-to-surge-in-activism/ar-AAxFfLk?ocid=spartandhp&ffid=gz

Juvonen, J. (2001). School violence: Prevalence, fears and prevention. *Rand Corporation.* Retrieved from https://www.rand.org/pubs/issue_papers/IP219/index2.html

K12 Academics. (2018). *History of school shootings in the United States.* Retrieved from http://www.k12academics.com/school-shootings/history-school-shootings-united-states#.WqfL-kxFzy0

Kamenetz, A. (2016). *When teacher take a breath, students can bloom.* Retrieved from https://www.npr.org/sections/ed/2016/08/19/488866975/when-teachers-take-a-breath-students-can-bloom

Kamenetz, A. (2018). *What 'A Nation at Risk' got wrong, and right, about U.S. schools.* Retrieved from https://www.npr.org/sections/ed/2018/04/29/604986823/what-a-nation-at-risk-got-wrong-and-right-about-u-s-schools

Kamerman, D., & Blumenthal, K. (2018). For safe schools, give students the support they need. Retrieved from https://www.lohud.com/story/opinion/contributors/2018/05/02/safe-schools-student-support/566559002/

Kaufman, J. (2013). *A trauma-informed school*. Retrieved from http://traumaawareschools.org/articles/transcript/9563

Kiehl, K.A., & Hoffman, M.B. (2011). The criminal psychopath: History, neuroscience, treatment, and economics. *Jurimetrics, 51*, 355–397. Retrieved from https://www.ncbi.nlm.nih.gov/pmc/articles/PMC4059069/

Klein, J. (2012). *The bully society: School shootings and the crisis of bulling in America's schools*. New York: New York University Press.

Klevens, J. (2011). Collective violence and children. In R.E. Tremblay, M. Boivin, & RDeV. Peters (Eds.), *Encyclopedia on early childhood development* [online]. Retrieved from http://www.child-encyclopedia.com/social-violence/according-experts/collective-violence-and-children

Knightsmith, P., Treasure, J., & Schmidt, U. (2013). Spotting and supporting eating disorders in school: Recommendations from school staff. *Health Education Research, 28*(6), 1004–1013. DOI: 10.1093/her/cyt080

Konnikova, M. (2014). Is there a link between mental health and gun violence? *The New Yorker*, November 19, 2014. Retrieved from https://www.newyorker.com/science/maria-konnikova/almost-link-mental-health-gun-violence

Korte, L. (2017). *Youth suicide rates are rising: School and the internet may be to blame*. Retrieved from https://www.usatoday.com/story/news/nation-now/2017/05/30/youth-suicide-rates-rising-school-and-internet-may-blame/356539001/

Kosciw, J.G., Greytak, E.A., Giga, N.M., Villenas, C., & Danischewski, D.J. (2015). *The 2015 national school climate survey: The experiences of lesbian, gay, bisexual, transgender, and queer youth in our nation's schools*. Retrieved from https://www.glsen.org/article/2015-national-school-climate-survey

Kraus, H.H. (2005). Conceptualizing violence. In F. Denmark, H.H. Kraus, R. Wesner, E. Midlarsky, & U.P. Gilen (Eds.), *Violence in schools: Cross-national and cross-cultural perspectives*, 11–34. DOI: 10.1007/0-387-28811-2

Krug, E.G., Mercy, J.A., Dahlberg, L.L., & Zwi, A.B. (2002). The world report on violence and health. *World Health Organization*. DOI: 10.1016/S0140-6736(02)11133-0

Kutner, M. (2018). Teen suicide is contagious, and the problem may be worse than we thought. Retrieved from http://www.newsweek.com/2016/10/28/teen-suicide-contagious-colorado-springs-511365.html

Lang, N. (2018). New study: Rates of anti-LGBTQ school bullying at 'unprecedented high'. Retrieved from https://www.thedailybeast.com/new-study-rates-of-anti-lgbtq-school-bullying-at-unprecedented-high

Langman, P. (2009). *Why kids kill: Inside the minds of school shooters*. New York, NY: St. Martin's Griffin.

Langman, P. (2015). *School shooters: Understanding high school, college, and adult perpetrators*. Lanham, MD: Rowman & Littlefield.

Larmer, J., Mergendoller, J., & Boss, S. (2015). *Setting the standard for project-based learning: A proven approach to rigorous classroom instruction*. Alexandria, VA: ASCD.

Lazzaro, B., Brock, S.E., & Dwyer, K. (2014). *Mentally healthy school crisis prevention & intervention*. Retrieved from https://www.cmhnetwork.org/news/mentally-health-school-crisis-training

Learning Never Stops. (2012). *School shootings: Prevalence, cases and possible prevention strategies based on empirical evidence.* Retrieved from https://learningneverstops.wordpress.com/2012/12/19/school_shooting/

Leary, M., Kowalski, R.M., Smith, L., & Phillips, S. (2003). Teasing, rejection, and violence: Case studies of the school shootings. *Aggressive Behavior, 29*(3), 202–214. Retrieved from https://onlinelibrary.wiley.com/doi/full/10.1002/ab.10061

Lewis, S. (2009). *Improving school climate: Findings from schools implementing restorative practices.* Retrieved from https://www.iirp.edu/pdf/IIRP-Improving-School-Climate-2009.pdf

Lewis, T., & Sugai, G. (2008). *Including all students and positive school culture.* Philadelphia, PA: OSEP Center on PBIS.

Liang, B., & Spencer, R. (2013). *21st century Athenas: Aligning achievement and well- being.* Retrieved from http://www.21stcenturyathenas.org

Liu, L. (2016). *Study reveals LGBT students face unprecedented violence in high schools nationwide.* Retrieved from http://www.businessinsider.com/lgbt-high-school-students-face-violence-nationwide-2016-8

Long, C. (2012). *Bullying of teachers pervasive in many schools.* Retrieved from http://neatoday.org/2012/05/16/bullying-of-teachers-pervasive-in-many-schools-2/

Loschert, K. (2016). *The suspension effect: Exclusionary discipline practices increase high school dropout rates and cost the nation billions in lost tax revenue, according to the Center for Civil Rights Remedies.* Retrieved from https://all4ed.org/articles/the-suspension-effect-exclusionary-discipline-practices-increase-high-school-dropout-rates-and-cost-the-nation-billions-in-lost-tax-revenue-according-to-the-center-for-civil-rights-remedies/

Luthar, S.S. (2003). The culture of affluence: Psychological costs of material wealth. *Child Development, 74*(6), 1581–1593. Retrieved from https://www.ncbi.nlm.nih.gov/pmc/articles/PMC1950124/

Mahnken, K. (2017). *The hidden mental health crisis in America's schools: Millions of kids not receiving services they need.* Retrieved from https://www.realcleareducation.com/2017/11/08/the_hidden_mental_health_crisis_in_america039s_schools_45372.html

Martin, D.C. (2013). Teachers' perceptions and satisfaction with PBIS in a Southwest Georgia school district. Retrieved from https://digitalcommons.georgiasouthern.edu/cgi/viewcontent.cgi?referer=https://www.google.com/&httpsredir=1&article=1885&context=etd

Maslow, A.H. (1987). *Motivation and personality* (3rd ed.). New Delhi: Pearson.

Mass-Galloway, R., Panyan, M., Smith, C., & Wessendorf, S. (2008). Systems change with school-wide behavior supports Iowa's work in progress. *Journal of Positive Behavior Interventions, 10*(2), 129–135. DOI: 10.1177/1098300707312545

Masten, A.S. (2018). Resilience theory and research on children and families: Past, present and promise. *Journal of Family Theory & Review, 10*(1), 12–31. DOI: 10.1111/jftr.12255

Maynard, B.R., Vaughn, M.G., Salas-Wright, C.P., & Vaughn, S.R. (2016). Bullying victimization among school-aged immigrant youth in the United States. *Journal of Adolescent Health, 58*(3), 337–344. DOI: 10.1016/j.jadohealth.2015.11.013

McBride, D.L. (2016). Young adolescents as likely to die from suicide as from traffic accidents. *Journal of Pediatrics, 32,* 83–84. DOI: 10.1016/j.pedn.2016.11.006

McInerney, M., & McKlindon, A. (2015). *Unlocking the door to learning: Trauma-informed classrooms & transformational Schools.* Retrieved from https://www.elc-pa.org/wp-content/uploads/2015/06/Trauma-Informed-in-Schools-Classrooms-FINAL-December2014-2.pdf

McKay, T., Misra, S., & Lindquist, C. (2017). Violence and LGBTQ+ communities: What do we know, and what do we need to know? *RTI International.* Retrieved from https://www.rti.org/sites/default/files/rti_violence_and_lgbtq_communities.pdf

McMahon, J. (2016). *US schools turn to yoga, meditation instead of detention, suspension.* Retrieved from http://www.syracuse.com/schools/index.ssf/2016/09/schools_turn_to_yoga_meditation_instead_of_detention_suspension.html

Mekouar, D. (2018). *Will Parkland student activists define America's younger generation?* Retrieved from https://learningenglish.voanews.com/a/will-parkland-student-activists-define-america-s-younger-generation-/4417834.html

Merriam Webster Dictionary. (n.d.). *Definition of violence.* Retrieved from https://www.merriam-webster.com/dictionary/violence

Midlarsky, E., & Klain, H.M. (2005). A history of violence in the schools. In F. Denmark, H.H. Kraus, R.W. Wesner, E. Midlarsky, & U.P. Gielen (Eds.). *Violence in schools: Cross-national and cross-cultural perspectives.* DOI: 10.1007/0-387-28811-2

Miller, W. (1975). Violence by youth gangs and youth groups as a crime problem in major American cities. Retrieved from https://www.ncjrs.gov/pdffiles1/Digitization/34497NCJRS.pdf

Miller, F.G., Cohen, D., Chafouleas, S.M., Riley-Tillman, T.C., Welsh, M.E., & Fabiano, G.A. (2015). A comparison of measures to screen for social, emotional, and behavioral risk. *School Psychology Quarterly, 30*(2), 184–196. DOI: 10.1037/spq0000085

Mindfulness in Schools Project. (2018). *A lifelong toolkit for children.* Retrieved from https://mindfulnessinschools.org/

MindMatters. (n.d.). *What is MindMatters?* Retrieved from https://www.mindmatters.edu.au/about-mindmatters/what-is-mindmatters

Moran, K. (2016). Anxiety in the classroom: Implications for middle school teachers. *Middle School Journal, 47*(1), 27–32. DOI: 10.1080/00940771.2016.1059727

National Alliance on Mental Illness [NAMI]. (2013). *State legislation report 2013: Trends, themes & best practices in state mental health legislation.* Retrieved from https://www.nami.org/getattachment/About-NAMI/Publications/Reports/2013StateLegislationReportFinal.pdf

National Alliance on Mental Illness [NAMI]. (2018). Ending the silence. Retrieved from https://www.nami.org/Find-Support/NAMI-Programs/NAMI-Ending-the-Silence

NASP School Safety and Crisis Response Committee. (2014). *Threat assessment for school administrators and crisis teams.* Retrieved from https://www.nasponline.org/resources-and-publications/resources/school-safety-and-crisis/threat-assessment-at-school/threat-assessment-for-school-administrators-and-crisis-teams

NASP School Safety and Crisis Response Committee. (2015). *Responding to school violence prevention: Guidelines for school administrators and crisis teams.* Retrieved from https://www.nasponline.org/resources-and-publications/resources/school-safety-and-crisis/school-violence-prevention/responding-to-school-violence-tips-for-administrators

National Association of School Psychologists [NASP]. (2013a). *PREPaRE school crisis prevention and intervention training curriculum.* Retrieved from https://pdfs.semanticscholar.org/presentation/2d54/45ce4a53a05389094f0ffdd3df295116ea063.pdf

National Association of School Psychologists [NASP]. (2013b). *Rethinking school safety: Communities and schools working together.* Retrieved from https://www.nasponline.org/research-and-policy/current-law-and-policy-priorities/briefings/rethinking-school-safety-schools-and-communities-working-together

National Association of School Psychologists [NASP]. (2017). Threat assessment for school administrators and crisis teams. Retrieved from https://www.nasponline.org/resources-and-publications/resources/school-safety-and-crisis/threat-assessment-at-school/threat-assessment-for-school-administrators-and-crisis-teams

National Gang Center. (n.d.). *Promoting alternative thinking strategies.* Retrieved from https://www.nationalgangcenter.gov/SPT/Programs/104

National SAVE. (2017). *SAVE promise clubs: Who we are.* Retrieved from http://nationalsave.org/who-we-are/

National School Safety and Security Services. (2018). *Best practices for school security and emergency preparedness planning.* Retrieved from http://www.schoolsecurity.org/trends/best-practices-for-school-security-and-emergency-preparedness-planning/

New Harbinger. (2015). *Relational teaching approaches to boost student engagement.* Retrieved from https://www.newharbinger.com/blog/relational-teaching-approaches-boost-student-engagement

Ngui, E.M., Khasakhala, L., Ndetei, D., & Roberts, L.W. (2010). Mental disorders, health inequalities and ethics: A global perspective. *International Review of Psychiatry, 22*(3), 235–244. DOI: 10.3109/09540261.2010.485273

O'Connell, M.E., Boat, T., & Warner, K.E. (2009). *Preventing mental, emotional, and behavioral disorders among young people: Progress and possibilities.* Washington, DC: The National Academies Press. DOI: 10.17226/12480

O'Connor, E.E., Dearing, E., & Collins, B.A. (2011). Teacher-child relationship and behavior problem trajectories in elementary school. *American Educational Research Journal, 48*(1), 120–162. DOI: 10.3102/0002831210365008

Ortega, L., Lyubansky, M., Nettles, S., & Espelage, D.L. (2016). Outcomes of a restorative circles program in a high school setting. *Psychology of Violence, 6*(3), 459–468. DOI: 10.1037/vio0000048

Owen, J., Wettach, J., & Hoffman, K.C. (2015). *Instead of suspension: Alternative strategies for effective school discipline.* Retrieved from https://law.duke.edu/childedlaw/schooldiscipline/downloads/instead_of_suspension.pdf

Page, D. (2017). *Five things schools can do to help pupils' mental health.* Retrieved from https://theconversation.com/five-things-schools-can-do-to-help-pupils-mental-health-79376

Palumbo, J.S. (2016). *Strain and the school shooter: A theoretical approach to the offender's perspective.* Retrieved from https://encompass.eku.edu/cgi/viewcontent.cgi?article=1408&context=etd

Paolini, A. (2015). *School shootings and student mental health: Role of the school counselor in mitigating violence.* Retrieved from https://www.counseling.org/docs/default-source/vistas/school-shootings-and-student-mental-health.p

Parker, J., & Folkman, J. (2015). Building resilience in students at the intersection of special education and foster care: Challenges, strategies, and resources for educators. *Issues in Teacher Education, 24*(2), 43–62. Retrieved from https://files.eric.ed.gov/fulltext/EJ1090358.pdf

Pekarsky, A.R. (2018). *Overview of child maltreatment. Merck Manual: Professional Version.* Retrieved from https://www.merckmanuals.com/professional/pediatrics/child-maltreatment/overview-of-child-maltreatment

Peterson, T. (2018a). *What causes mental illness? Genetics, environment, risk factors.* Retrieved from https://www.healthyplace.com/other-info/mental-illness-overview/what-causes-mental-illness-genetics-environment-risk-factors

Peterson, T. (2018b). *Mental illness in children: Types, symptoms, treatments.* Retrieved from https://www.healthyplace.com/other-info/mental-illness-overview/mental-illness-in-children-types-symptoms-treatments

Pfeifer, B., & Ganzevoort, R.R. (2014). The implicit religion of school shootings: Existential concerns of perpetrators prior to their crime. *Journal of Religion and Violence, 2*(30), 447–459. DOI: 10.5840/jrv20153172

Pickens, I.B., & Tschopp, N. (2017). *Trauma-informed classrooms.* Retrieved from https://www.ncjfcj.org/sites/default/files/NCJFCJ_SJP_Trauma_Informed_Classrooms_Final.pdf

Pipe, L. (2014). *Mental health and safety in schools: Children's perceptions and experiences.* Electronic Thesis and Dissertation Repository, https://ir.lib.uwo.ca/etd/1931

Pitner, R.O., Marachi, R., Astor, R.A., & Benbenishty, R. (2015). Evidence-based violence prevention programs and best implementation practices. In A.R. Roberts (Ed.), *Social worker's desk reference,* 3–26. New York, NY: Oxford University Press.

Pollack, W. (1998). *Real boys: Rescuing our sons from the myths of boyhood.* New York, NY: Holt.

Pollack, W. (2000). *Real boys' voices: Boys speak out about drugs, sex, violence, bullying, sports, girls, school, parents and so much more.* New York, NY: Penguin.

Positive Behavioral Interventions & Supports [PBIS]. (2018). *What is school-wide PBIS?* Retrieved https://www.pbis.org/school

Quinn, M.M. (2018). Gender, work, & health. *Annals of Work Exposures and Health, 62*(4), 516. DOI: 10.1093/annweh/wxy027

Rachel's Challenge. (n.d.a). *About us.* Retrieved from https://rachelschallenge.org/about-us

Rachel's Challenge. (n.d.b). *Middle school/high school program.* Retrieved from https://rachelschallenge.org/programs/middle-school-high-school

Rachel's Challenge. (n.d.c). *Elementary programs.* Retrieved from https://rachels challenge.org/programs/elementary

Rahim, H. (2015). *Three powerful messages for promoting mental health awareness in every school.* Retrieved from https://www.nami.org/blogs/nami-blog/april-2015/three-powerful-messages-for-promoting-mental-health

Reichert, M., & Hawley, R. (2013). Relationships play primary role in boys' learning. *Phi Delta Kappan, 94*(8), 49–53. DOI: 10.1177/003172171309400812

Reinemann, D.H.S., & Teeter Ellison, P.A. (2008). The role of internal and external protective factors in low-income, ethnic minority children's psychological reactions to community violence exposure. *Journal of Child & Adolescent Trauma, 1*(1), 23–45. DOI: 10.1080/19361520801929852

Restorative Justice Council [RJC]. (2011). *Best practice guidance for restorative practice.* Retrieved from https://restorativejustice.org.uk/sites/default/files/resources/files/Best%20practice%20guidance%20for%20restorative%20practice%202011.pdf

Riggio, O. (2018). *Mental illness serves as easy scapegoat in mass murder accounts.* Retrieved from https://fair.org/home/mental-illness-serves-as-easy-scapegoat-in-mass-murder-accounts/

Rock, A. (2018). New study: Significant rise in suicide attempts among kids, teens. *Campus Safety.* Retrieved from https://www.campussafetymagazine.com/safety/suicide-attempts-kids-teens/

Rothschild, A.J. (2013). Challenges in the treatment of major depressive disorder with psychotic features. *Schizophrenia Bulletin, 39*(4), 787–796. DOI: 10.1093/schbul/sbt046

Rollison, J., Banks, D., Martin, A.J., Owens, C., Thomas, N., Dressler, K.J., & Wells, M. (2013). Improving school-justice partnerships: Lessons learned from the safe schools/healthy students initiative. *Family Court Review, 51*, 445–451. DOI: 10.1111/fcre/12041

Rosen, P. (2018). *MTSS: What you need to know.* Retrieved from https://www.understood.org/en/learning-attention-issues/treatments-approaches/educational-strategies/mtss-what-you-need-to-know

Rosenberg, M. (2003). *Life-enriching education: Non-violent communication helps schools improve performance, reduce conflict, and enhance relationships.* Encinitas, CA: Puddle Dancer Press.

Rosin, H. (2015). *The Silicon Valley suicides: Why are so many kids with bright prospects killing themselves in Palo Alto?* Retrieved from https://www.theatlantic.com/magazine/archive/2015/12/the-silicon-valley-suicides/413140/

Ross, K. (2017). *School based interventions for school-aged children with oppositional defiant disorder: A systematic review.* Retrieved from https://sophia.stkate.edu/cgi/viewcontent.cgi?article=1787&context=msw_papers

Runyowa, S. (2015). *Microaggressions matter.* Retrieved from https://www.theatlantic.com/politics/archive/2015/09/microaggressions-matter/406090/

Rutter, M. (1986). Psychosocial resilience and protective mechanisms. *American Journal of Orthropsychiarty, 57*(3). DOI: 10.1111/j.1939-0025.1987.tb035411.x

Sadker, M., & Sadker, D. (1994). *Failing at fairness: How America's schools cheat girls.* New York, NY: Maxwell Macmillan.

Safe and Sound Schools. (2016). *The connection between mental health and school safety.* Retrieved from https://www.safeandsoundschools.org/2016/05/23/the-connection-between-mental-health-school-safety/

Sagor, R. (1996). Building resiliency in students. *Educational Leadership, 54*(1), 38–43. http://www.ascd.org/publications/educational-leadership/sept96/vol54/num01/Building-Resiliency-in-Students.aspx

Scott, D., & Marzano, R. (2014). *Awaken the learner: Finding the source of effective education.* Bloomington, IN: Marzano Research.

Smith, P.K., Morita, Y., Junger-Tas, J., Catalano, D., Olweus, R., & Slee, P. (1999). *The nature of school bullying: A cross-national perspective.* New York, NY: Routledge.

Substance Abuse and Mental Health Services Administration [SAMHSA]. (2018). *Risk and protective factors.* Retrieved from https://www.samhsa.gov/capt/programs-campaigns/center-application-prevention-technologies/practicing-effective-prevention-2

Shapiro, H.S., & Purpel, D.E. (Eds.) (2004). *Critical social issues in American education: Democracy and meaning in a globalizing world.* Mahway, NJ: Lawrence Erlbaum Associates.

Sicart, M. (2009). *The ethics computer games.* Retrieved from https://is.muni.cz/el/1421/jaro2014/IM090/Miguel_Sicart_The_Ethics_of_Computer_Games_2009.pdf

Simidian, G. (2017). *Rethinking school discipline.* Retrieved from https://www.nyssba.org/clientuploads/nyssba_pdf/rethinking-school-discipline-04272017.pdf

Smokowski, P.R., Cotter, K.L., Robertson, C., & Guo, S. (2013). Demographic, psychological, and school environment correlates of bullying victimization and school hassles in rural youth. *Journal of Criminology.* DOI: 10.1155/2013/137583

St. George, D. (2016). *How mindfulness practices are changing an inner-city school.* Retrieved from https://www.washingtonpost.com/local/education/how-mindfulness-practices-are-changing-an-inner-city-school/2016/11/13/7b4a274a-a833-11e6-ba59-a7d93165c6d4_story.html?utm_term=.217a1372eae3

Steffgen, G., Recchia, S., & Viechtbauer, W. (2013). The link between school climate and violence in school: A meta-analytic review. *Aggression and Violent Behavior, 18*(2), 300–309. DOI: 10.1016/j.avb.2012.12.001

Stewart, C., & Mohandie, K. (2014). *Threat assessment: Evaluating risk of targeted violence.* Retrieved from http://www.theiacp.org/Portals/0/documents/pdfs/PSYCH2014_ThreatAssessment.pdf

Strauss, V. (2013). *Obama's proposals on school safety.* Retrieved from https://www.washingtonpost.com/news/answer-sheet/wp/2013/01/16/obamas-proposals-on-school-safety/?utm_term=.3a442df9355b

Strong, M. (2016). *Are public schools causing an epidemic of mental illness?* Retrieved from https://medium.com/@flowidealism/are-public-schools-causing-an-epidemic-of-mental-illness-1b37b6c0ef3e

Sue, D.W. (2010). *Microaggressions: More than just race*. Retrieved from https://www.psychologytoday.com/us/blog/microaggressions-in-everyday-life/201011/microaggressions-more-just-race

Swanson, J.W. (2011). Explaining rare acts of violence: The limits of evidence from population research. *Psychiatric Services, 62*(11), 1369–1371.

Swanson, J., Easter, M.M., Robertson, A.G., Swartz, M.S., Alanis-Hirsch, K., Moseley, D. Dion, C., & Petrila, J. (2016). *Study of 81,000 adults examines mental illness, gun violence and suicide*. Retrieved form https://medschool.duke.edu/about-us/news-and-communications/med-school-blog/study-81000-adults-examines-mental-illness-gun-violence-and-suicide

Swanson, J.W., McGinty, E., Fazel, S., & Mays, V.M. (2015). Mental illness and reduction of gun violence and suicide: Bringing epidemiologic research to policy. *Annals of Epidemiology, 25*, 366–376. DOI: 10.1016/j.annepidem.2014.03.004

Szalavitz, M. (2012). How child abuse primes the brain for future mental illness. *Time*. Retrieved from http://healthland.time.com/2012/02/15/how-child-abuse-primes-the-brain-for-future-mental-illness/

Szalavitz, M. (2013). Abused children may get unique form of PTSD. *Time*. Retrieved from http://healthland.time.com/2013/04/30/abused-children-may-get-different-form-of-ptsd/

The National Child Traumatic Stress Network [NCTSN]. (n.d.a). *What is child trauma?* Retrieved from https://www.nctsn.org/what-is-child-trauma/about-child-trauma

The National Child Traumatic Stress Network [NCTSN]. (n.d.b). *About child trauma*. Retrieved from https://www.nctsn.org/what-is-child-trauma/about-child-trauma

Tough, P. (2016). *How kids learn resilience*. Retrieved from https://www.theatlantic.com/magazine/archive/2016/06/how-kids-really-succeed/480744/

Towvim, L., Anderson, K., Thomas, B., & Blaisdell, A. (2012). *Positive behavioral interventions and supports: A snapshot from safe schools/healthy students initiatives*. Retrieved from http://sshs.promoteprevent.org/sites/default/files/pbis_32813.pdf

Twenge, J.M. (2012). Yes, violent video games do cause aggression: So why do some say otherwise? *Psychology Today*. Retrieved from https://www.psychologytoday.com/us/blog/our-changing-culture/201212/yes-violent-video-games-do-cause-aggression

United Nations Educational, Scientific and Cultural Organization. (2017). *School violence and bullying: Global status report*. Retrieved from http://unesdoc.unesco.org/images/0024/002469/246970e.pdf

U.S. Department of Education. (2016). *Practical information on crisis planning brochure*. Retrieved from https://www2.ed.gov/admins/lead/safety/crisisplanning.html

U.S. Department of Education, Office for Civil Rights. (2015). *Title IX and sex discrimination*. Retrieved from https://www2.ed.gov/about/offices/list/ocr/docs/tix_dis.html?exp=0

U.S. Department of Health & Human Services: Mental Health. (2017). *Mental health myths and facts*. Retrieved from https://www.mentalhealth.gov/basics/mental-health-myths-facts

von der Embse, N.P., & Witmer, S.E. (2014). High stakes accountability: Student anxiety and large-scale testing. *Journal of Applied School Psychology, 30*(2), 132–156. DOI: 10.1080/15377903.2014.888529

Wachtel, T. (2016). *Defining restorative.* Retrieved from https://www.iirp.edu/images/pdf/Defining-Restorative_Nov-2016.pdf

Wadman, R., Glazebrook, C., Parkes, E., & Jackson, G.M. (2014). Supporting students with Tourette syndrome in secondary school: A survey of staff views. *Journal of Special Educational Needs, 16*(4). DOI: 10.1111/1471-3802.12077

Walker, T. (2013a). *Violence against teachers: An overlooked crisis.* Retrieved from http://neatoday.org/2013/02/19/violence-against-teachers-an-overlooked-crisis-2/

Walker, T. (2013b). *Is mental health the next focus of the school safety debate?* Retrieved from http://neatoday.org/2013/12/13/is-mental-health-the-next-focus-of-the-school-safety-debate/

Walkley, M., & Cox, T.L. (2013). Building trauma-informed schools and communities. *Children and Schools, 35*(1), 123–126. DOI: 10.1093/cs/cdt007

Warner, E.E., & Smith, R.S. (1982). *Vulnerable but invincible: A longitudinal study of resilient children and youth.* New York, NY: McGraw-Hill.

Waters, J.T., & Marzano, R.J. (2006). School district leadership that works: The effect of superintendent leadership on student achievement. *Mid-Continent Research for Education and Learning.* Retrieved from https://eric.ed.gov/?id=ED494270

Weare, K., & Gray, G. (2003). What works in developing children's emotional and social competence and well-being? Retrieved from http://learning.gov.wales/docs/learningwales/publications/121129emotionalandsocialcompetenceen.pdf

Weir, K. (2012). The roots of mental illness: How much of mental illness can the biology of the brain explain? *American Psychological Association, 43*(6), 30. Retrieved from http://www.apa.org/monitor/2012/06/roots.aspx

Werner, E.E., & Smith, R.S. (1982). *Vulnerable but invincible: A study of resilient children.* New York, NY: McGraw-Hill.

Werner, E.E., & Smith, R.S. (1992). *Overcoming the odds: High risk children from birth to adulthood.* Ithaca, NY: Cornell University Press.

Wilke, T.L., & Fraser, M.W. (2009). School shootings: Making sense of the senseless. *Aggression and Violent Behavior*, 162–169. DOI: 10.1016/j.avb.2009.01.005

Wolfe, P. (2010). *Brain Matters: Translating research into classroom practice.* Alexandria, VA: ASCD

Workplace Bullying Institute [WBI]. (2018). *2017 WBI U.S. workplace bullying survey: June 2017.* Retrieved from https://www.workplacebullying.org/wbiresearch/wbi-2017-survey/

World Health Organization [WHO]. (2003). *Creating an environment for emotional and social well-being.* Retrieved from apps.who.int/iris/handle/10665/42819

World Health Organization [WHO]. (2016). *Youth violence: Fact sheet.* Retrieved from http://www.who.int/news-room/fact-sheets/detail/youth-violence

World Health Organization [WHO]. (2017). *Violence against women.* Retrieved from http://www.who.int/news-room/fact-sheets/detail/violence-against-women

World Health Organization [WHO]. (2018). *Definition and typology of violence.* Retrieved from http://www.who.int/violenceprevention/approach/definition/en/

Wyn, J., Cahill, H., Holdsworth, R., Rowling, L., & Carson, S. (2000). MindMatters, a whole-school approach promoting mental health and wellbeing. *Australian and New Zealand Journal of Psychiatry, 34*(4), 594–601. DOI: 10.1080/j.1440-1614.2000.00748.x

Wyss, S.E. (2004). This was my 'hell': The violence experienced by gender nonconforming youth in US high schools. *International Journal of Qualitative Studies in Education, 17*(5), 709–730. DOI: 10.1080/0951839042000236676

Young, N.D., Bonanno-Sotiropoulos, K., & Mumby, M.A. (2019). *Embracing and educating the autistic child: Valuing those who color outside the lines.* Lanham, MD: Roman & Littlefield.

Zakrzewski, V. (2013). *How to create a positive school climate.* Retrieved from https ://greatergood.berkeley.edu/article/item/how_to_create_a_positive_sch

About the Authors

Dr. Nicholas D. Young has worked in diverse educational roles for more than thirty years, serving as a principal, special education director, graduate professor, graduate program director, graduate dean, and longtime superintendent of schools. He was named the Massachusetts Superintendent of the Year; and he completed a distinguished Fulbright program focused on the Japanese educational system through the collegiate level. Dr. Young is the recipient of numerous other honors and recognitions including the General Douglas MacArthur Award for distinguished civilian and military leadership and the Vice Admiral John T. Hayward Award for exemplary scholarship. He holds several graduate degrees including a PhD in educational administration and an EdD in educational psychology.

Dr. Young has served in the U.S. Army and U.S. Army Reserves combined for over thirty-four years; and he graduated with distinction from the U.S. Air War College, the U.S. Army War College, and the U.S. Navy War College. After completing a series of senior leadership assignments in the U.S. Army Reserves as the commanding officer of the 287th Medical Company (DS), the 405th Area Support Company (DS), the 405th Combat Support Hospital, and the 399th Combat Support Hospital, he transitioned to his current military position as a faculty instructor at the U.S. Army War College in Carlisle, PA. He currently holds the rank of Colonel.

Dr. Young is also a regular presenter at state, national, and international conferences; and he has written many books, book chapters, and/or articles on various topics in education, counseling, and psychology. Some of his most recent books include *Securing the Schoolyard: Protocols that Promote Safety and Positive Student Behaviors* (in-press); *The Soul of the Schoolhouse: Cultivating Student Engagement* (2019); *Embracing and Educating the Autistic Child: Valuing Those Who Color Outside the Lines* (2019);

From Cradle to Classroom: A Guide to Special Education for Young Children (2019); *Captivating Classrooms: Student Engagement at the Heart of School Improvement* (2019); *Potency of the Principalship: Action-Oriented Leadership at the Heart of School Improvement* (2018); *Soothing the Soul: Pursuing a Life of Abundance Through a Practice of Gratitude* (2018); *Dog Tags to Diploma: Understanding and Addressing the Educational Needs of Veterans, Servicemembers, and their Families* (2018); *Turbulent Times: Confronting Challenges in Emerging Adulthood* (2018); *Guardians of the Next Generation: Igniting the Passion for Quality Teaching* (2018); *Achieving Results: Maximizing Success in the Schoolhouse* (2018); *From Head to Heart: High Quality Teaching Practices in the Spotlight* (2018); *Stars in the Schoolhouse: Teaching Practices and Approaches that Make a Difference* (2018); *Making the Grade: Promoting Positive Outcomes for Students with Learning Disabilities* (2018); *Paving the Pathway for Educational Success: Effective Classroom Interventions for Students with Learning Disabilities* (2018); *Wrestling with Writing: Effective Strategies for Struggling Students* (2018); *Floundering to Fluent: Reaching and Teaching the Struggling Student* (2018); *Emotions and Education: Promoting Positive Mental Health in Students with Learning* (2018); *From Lecture Hall to Laptop: Opportunities, Challenges, and the Continuing Evolution of Virtual Learning in Higher Education* (2017); *The Power of the Professoriate: Demands, Challenges, and Opportunities in 21st Century Higher Education* (2017); *To Campus with Confidence: Supporting a Successful Transition to College for Students with Learning Disabilities* (2017); *Educational Entrepreneurship: Promoting Public-Private Partnerships for the 21st Century* (2015); *Beyond the Bedtime Story: Promoting Reading Development during the Middle School Years* (2015); *Betwixt and Between: Understanding and Meeting the Social and Emotional Developmental Needs of Students During the Middle School Transition Years* (2014); *Learning Style Perspectives: Impact Upon the Classroom* (3rd ed., 2014); and *Collapsing Educational Boundaries from Preschool to PhD: Building Bridges Across the Educational Spectrum* (2013); *Transforming Special Education Practices: A Primer for School Administrators and Policy Makers* (2012); and *Powerful Partners in Student Success: Schools, Families and Communities* (2012). He also coauthored several children's books, including the popular series *I am Full of Possibilities*. Dr. Young may be contacted directly at nyoung1191@aol.com.

Dr. Christine N. Michael is a more than 40-year educational veteran with a variety of professional experiences. She holds degrees from Brown University, Rhode Island College, Union Institute and University, and the University of Connecticut, where she earned a PhD in education, human development, and family relations. Her previous work has included middle and high school teaching, higher education administration, college teaching, and educational consulting. She has also been involved with Head Start, Upward Bound, national non-profits Foundation for Excellent Schools and College for Every Student, and the federal Trio programs. She is currently the Program Director of Low Residency Programs at American International College.

Dr. Michael has published widely on topics in education and psychology. Her most recent works included serving as a primary author on the book *Securing the Schoolyard: Protocols that Promote Safety and Positive Student Behaviors* (in-press); *The Soul of the Schoolhouse: Cultivating Student Engagement* (2019); *Captivating Classrooms: Student Engagement at the Heart of School Improvement* (2019); *Turbulent Times: Confronting Challenges in Emerging Adulthood* (2018); *To Campus with Confidence: Supporting a Successful Transition to College for Students with Learning Disabilities* (2017); *Beyond the Bedtime Story: Promoting Reading Development during the Middle School Years* (2015); *Betwixt and Between: Understanding and Meeting the Social and Emotional Development Needs of Students During the Middle School Transition Years* (2014); and *Powerful Partners in Student Success: Schools, Families and Communities* (2012). Dr. Michael may be contacted at cnevadam@gmail.com.

Attorney Jennifer A. Smolinski has worked in education for more than three years. Her role within higher education includes the creation of, and coordinator for, the Center for Accessibility Services and Academic Accommodations at American International College located in Springfield, Massachusetts. She has also taught criminal justice and legal research and writing classes within the field of higher education. Prior to her work at the collegiate level, Attorney Smolinski worked as a solo-practitioner conducting education and disability advocacy.

Attorney Smolinski holds several degrees including a law degree from Massachusetts School of Law. She is currently an EdD in Educational Leadership and Supervision candidate at American International College, where she is focusing her research on special education and laws to protect students with disabilities in the classroom.

Attorney Smolinski has become a regular presenter educating the faculty, staff and students at institutes of higher education on disabilities and accommodations at the collegiate level and has presented to local high school special education departments on the transition to college under the Americans with Disabilities Act. She has coauthored *Securing the Schoolyard: Protocols that Promote Safety and Positive Student Behaviors* (in-press); *The Soul of the Schoolhouse: Cultivating Student Engagement* (2019); *Captivating*

Classrooms: Student Engagement at the Heart of School Improvement (2019); *Guardian of the Next Generation: Igniting the Passion for Quality Teaching* (2018); and *Making the Grade: Promoting Positive Outcomes for Students with Learning Disabilities* (2018). She can be reached at Jennifer.Smolinski@aic.edu.

www.ingramcontent.com/pod-product-compliance
Lightning Source LLC
Chambersburg PA
CBHW030115010526
44116CB00005B/253